"To Hell with that!"

1986

"To Hell with that!"

or
The Life of
Oliver Gyles Longley,
C.B.E., M.C.

For Joure an John
with all Best Wishes

[signature]

The Grimsay Press

The Grimsay Press
An imprint of Zeticula Ltd
The Roan,
Kilkerran,
KA19 8LS,
Scotland
http://www.thegrimsaypress.co.uk

First published in 2012
Text and photographs © Gyles Longley 2012

Proceeds from the sale of this book will go
to the Royal British Legion, Paris Branch, Poppy Appeal
and
to Saint Michael's Anglican Church, Paris

ISBN 978-1-84530-127-9

To my sister Biddy
In memory of our Parents "Pop" and "The Old Lady"
and Brothers Charles and Dennis

After 45 years with Gestetner

Acknowledgements

I am much indebted to my sister Biddy for her input on the earlier period of our childhood and also to my nieces Diane Longley, R.A. (Design), and Sally Longley, as well as to my nephew Peter Hovenden Longley, M.A. (Cantab), for their encouragement and help over various family reminiscences, and to nephew Gyles Thomson for providing the text and relighting 'the coveted candlestick'.

My thanks, too, to my valiant friends Ilona Wicker, David Blanchard and Roy Mitchell for labouring through my text and for their abundant corrections.

Above all I am most grateful to my good friend Peter Howard for guiding me through the process of writing these memoirs, for correcting my text, and for putting me in touch with my editor and publisher, whose understanding of aged authors' memoirs has been most wise and comforting. But without Peter's constant encouragement I would never have written them at all. Peter's wife, Papychette, has been patient with both of us.

Whilst I have written mostly from memory, I have tried to keep on course by dipping into the various works mentioned in my bibliography as well as the occasional trawl through the internet to help me put dates and times into perspective but I am conscious there will still be some inaccuracies.

If I have, in reading about the Italian Campaign or elsewhere, retained in my memory or in my notes, a phrase or sentence which I inadvertently re-use, then I apologise.

Unfortunately my handwriting is now so bad I have had recourse to write these memoirs on my iMac with one finger of my left hand. This has been frustrating at times, particularly when Apple's logic does not coincide with mine. Steve Jobs always wins.

Introduction

"To Hell with that!" is not a denial of my life. I was eighteen at the time I uttered these words to mark my displeasure of a consultancy's report recommending my suitability for a career which did not appeal to me.

Whilst it is true I had not exactly excelled in my education at expensive schools, I felt I was worth more than that. My dignity and self respect had received a shock. As it happened, this marked the turning point when I came to realise that it was now up to me to make my way in the world.

I have always been close to my sister Biddy, but as I have spent most of my life abroad, and her life has mostly been spent in Scotland, we have not seen a great deal of each other. Not long ago she said she did not know much about what I have been doing all these years.

As I believe I have a story to tell which will interest Biddy, as well as other members of my family, and perhaps a wider circle, I decided to write my memoirs. Although my memory is good for my age, I regret I did not keep diaries and other notes which would have been helpful. I am aware therefore there are shortcomings and errors in my story, but I have tried to convey the essential.

I was lucky to be born into a wonderful family which brought me successfully through childhood and adolescence.

I have only spent about twenty-two years of my life in the United Kingdom. At eighteen I joined an internationally well-known British Company at their offices in London. At twenty I was sent to work for them in Europe for nearly two years until the outbreak of war. I was therefore a witness to the deteriorating international situation in all the major European countries, owing to the aggressive ambitions of Adolf Hitler, the German Chancellor.

At twenty-one I returned home to join the Army, spending my time learning to be a soldier, then an officer, and to help defend Britain against possible invasion after the evacuation from Dunkirk. At twenty-four I was posted overseas to take part in the North African Campaign from Alamein until the cessation of hostilities in that theatre. I took part in the Italian Campaign from Salerno until my demobilisation in Italy in 1946.

Wartime experience is an unforgetable adventure in the face of danger; the tragedy of the loss of comrades, the good and bad moments, responsibility and respect, and the ever present prospect of being maimed or losing one's life. My experience was no different nor more heroic than others, many of whom did not come home.

On my return to civilian life I was — almost immediately — invited to join the French subsidiary of the Company with whom I had been working pre-war. It was not an easy choice for me as I had been away from home for the past four years and would like to have stayed longer with my family and friends. Nevertheless my sense of adventure prevailed, so I accepted the offer and have lived in France ever since. My professional career was most rewarding. Above all, it was extremely satisfying in the excellent relationship I had with my French colleagues. For many years I was privileged to manage the French Company and later to be appointed to the Group Holdings Board.

At the age of thirty I was beginning to wonder if I would ever find the right person with whom to share my life. I then met Ginette, a charming vivacious girl. The best and most important episode of my life opened up before me when we married in 1949 and enjoyed fifty-seven wonderful years together.

Whilst my professional life was almost entirely conducted in French, our social life was more inclined towards the Franco-British community. It was a good mixture enabling us both to develop many interests and activities involving good relations between the two countries. Something which I have continued to do since my darling Ginette died in 2006.

Gyles Longley
July, 2012

Contents

Illustrations

Family Background

I was born on 30th September 1918, forty-two days before the Armistice of the Great World War, at my grandmother's house in Streatham, London, and named Oliver Gyles. I was christened into the Anglican tradition at Christchurch in Beckenham in Kent. After the 1914-1918 my father bought a house at 44, Manor Road, where my family came to live.

My father, Charles William Longley, married my mother, Catherine Amy Hovenden, in January 1914. Their first child was my elder brother, Charles William Hovenden Longley, born in 1915. After me came my sister Agnes Anna, always known as 'Biddy', born in 1919. My younger brother Dennis Southon was born in 1923.

My father had joined the Honorable Artillery Company (HAC) in 1913, and at the outbreak of the war was commissioned as an officer and transferred to the Royal Field Artillery (RFA) and left for France.

He was wounded in 1916 and transferred to the U.K., having been awarded the Military Cross. This award, which he received from King George V at Buckingham Palace in 1917, was created in 1914 for '*gallantry during active operations against the enemy*'. Father returned to France but was soon sent back to England with a serious kidney infection. He never went back to France again, remaining in England at Catterick Camp, the army school for signals, as an instructor in the rank of Captain.

Although it was never apparent at other times, my father must have suffered from his wartime experiences as he was

My father receiving his M.C. in 1917

often subject to severe nightmares, when he would cry out loudly and wake up with a start. However this 'disability' did not prevent him in any way from leading a perfectly normal family and business life.

The Longleys originated from Benenden in Kent and were farmers and butchers. On my mother's side, the Hovendens descended from Flemish weavers who settled around Cranbrook in Kent in the 14th Century. At that time King Edward III invited Flemish weavers from Louvain to the Weald of Kent to develop the weaving industry in this country in order to break the Flemish monopoly over the woollen cloth trade. Up till then Kentish wool was sent to Flanders to be converted into cloth which was then re-exported to England.

My grandfather, Oliver Longley, and my grandmother, Minnie, and family lived at Hillside, a big house in the Avenue, also at Beckenham, about eight miles from London. They had seven children, one of whom died at birth. My father Charles William was the eldest, my aunt Minnie Agnes came second. Uncles Oliver ('Tig'), George, my aunt Bernice, and finally Douglas followed.

Elizabeth Rendall (known as aunt Lig), my grandmother's sister, also lived with them. Never married, she was always very straight laced with decided standards of what was right or wrong. As was the custom at the time, spinsters or poorer relatives of a family helped with the upbringing of the children. Later, Aunt Lig looked after the grandchildren whenever they were at Hillside or the Breach, my grandfather's hobby farm. She also took on the task of keeping grandfather's suits brushed and clean, an uphill task as he was a heavy cigar smoker who dropped his ash onto his clothes, much to aunt Lig's disgust.

Like my grandfather, she was strictly teetotal until quite late in life, when her doctor recommended a little whisky would do her good. We were never quite sure if this had anything to do with her falling down stairs, resulting in her death. She lived to a good age, and had been a very faithful and devoted relative. A bit crusty, perhaps, and set in her ways, but she served the family so well over three generations.

I should mention here another very faithful servant of my grandparents, Kate Hudd.

Kate came to my grandparents as a scullery maid way back in time, becoming a housemaid and eventually the family cook. When I knew her, Kate was very much in charge of the kitchen. As grandchildren we loved to go to see her; she was always kind and cheerful. We also liked to go to the kitchen to see Polly, the family parrot. Polly arrived when my father was quite young. Nobody knew this parrot's age nor sex until quite late in its life, until Polly laid an egg. She was just as surprised as we all were by this strange event. She had laid the egg whilst on her perch, so it broke as it fell to the floor of the cage. Polly had quite a vocabulary. Having listened to Kate over so many years Polly regularly called 'Sewell, cup o'tea' to call the gardener in for his elevenses. She would say things like 'Kate, you silly old fool' and had many other phrases and words. Very often when she was in a loud chatty mood a cover had to be put over her cage to keep her quiet.

My great grandfather, Giles [sic] Longley was a book-keeper working for Campbell, a firm of wholesale meat salesmen in Smithfield Market in London. Eventually he became a partner and introduced his son Oliver, my grandfather, to this business.

Oliver Longley, in partnership with his great friend, Horace Key, took over Campbell's, becoming the firm of Campbell, Key & Longley, specialising in poultry and game. The business prospered well. When Horace Key died my grandfather became the sole owner. He acquired two other Smithfield businesses. R. F. Potter specialised in Scottish beef and lamb. E. Weatherley also specialised in poultry and game. Eventually my father and two of his brothers — uncles 'Tig' (Oliver) and George — entered these businesses, and also became partners. Father's brother Douglas, my elder brother

Charles, as well aunt Bernice's son, William Hayne also later entered the business. My niece, Diane, later joined Weatherlys as an accountant and, at the time of writing, still works there although the business no longer belongs to the family.

Diane is the fifth generation of Longleys in Smithfield. When I was quite young, a friend of my father's told me that as long as there is a Longley in the Market there will always be honesty. I was very proud. This was a wonderful mark of respect to my family and its principles. Although a diehard traditionalist in this respect, I think Diane is somewhat distressed with modern day business standards.

Shops in the Market are leased from the City of London, who are the owners of Smithfield. Hours were not easy for the family, as the Markets opened in the early hours of the morning.

My father would rise about three or four in the morning to walk, about ten minutes, to Beckenham Junction station to take the train to Holborn Viaduct, the station adjacent to Smithfield. Before leaving home he would make himself a cup of tea from a tea-making set in his bedroom. Often he would look into our bedrooms to see how we were. I was usually awake at these times so managed to cadge a small drink of tea. In fact, if I heard him stirring in the house, I would purposely keep myself awake in the hope he would look in and give me a 'cuppa'.

To shave he used an old fashioned 'cut-throat' razor which required constant stropping. He also dressed with a starched collar. Later, starched collars were no longer the fashion, and thanks to Mr Gillette safety razors came into being. Father would return in mid-afternoon when we would rush to try to be the first to find his slippers before teatime. Tea was quite a feast with bread and butter, sometimes scones, jam, and clotted cream, biscuits and homemade cake. In winter we toasted crumpets in front of the lounge fire using special toasting forks. Father invariably fell asleep after tea, or retired to his room for a rest before supper which would consist of soup, a meat dish with vegetables, or probably fish on Fridays, followed by a sweet, or perhaps a savoury dish.

Lunch was very much a meal for us children with stews, or minced meat dishes, with potatoes, plenty of green vegetables, puddings with custard or a junket. For breakfast we usually had porridge, or cereals, an egg dish with bacon, toast and tea.

On Saturdays and Sundays there was always a good choice of eggs, bacon, sausages, or grilled kidneys, or sweetbreads, sometimes kippers, or poached haddock for breakfast.

Naturally our meat was of the highest quality as it came directly from Smithfield, to be hung in the meat cellar at our house in Overbury Avenue, Beckenham. Invariably the Sunday joint was either a roast baron of beef or a saddle of mutton, served in a large dish with a well to collect the red gravy we all adored so much. This was followed by various suet puddings, rice puddings, or various fruit pies or tarts, custard and cream.

My mother was a late riser as she generally went to bed quite late, sometimes not much before my father got up. After supper my father would rapidly retire to bed whilst my mother took to playing patience, listening to the wireless, or talking to whoever might be around at the time. It was not an easy social life for both of them. My mother was involved in bringing us up and organising the running of the household. She was well occupied but later when we were either at school or growing up she was less happy with this routine until my father retired.

During their partnership Oliver and Horace also bought a hobby farm in Kent at Sarnden. When Horace Key died the farm was sold and grandfather bought another farm, the Breach Farm at Cranbrook, which my father acquired after grandfather's death in 1941. The farm later passed to my younger brother Dennis. The Breach was very much a family holiday home, not only for my father's generation but also for my generation of brothers and sister, several cousins and eventually their children. We spent many happy holidays there.

The farm workers lived in cottages on the estate. It was always our duty on arrival to go up to the cottages and pay our respects to Mrs Williams, the wife of the oldest farmworker, and to Mrs Collard whose husband was the foreman. They always received us so well with newly baked cakes in their beautifully kept cottages. Both Mrs Williams and Mrs Collard were good cooks and often stood in if required at the House.

The Breach provided eggs, milk and vegetables for the family. As my grandfather was not able to be present to manage the farm himself, it was managed by a local farmer friend. It was not a large estate — forty-eight acres, I believe. Mostly apple orchards, Cox's and Worcester Pearmains, some cherries, grazing for cattle, and pigs. Almost half the farm land was wooded with plenty of rabbits scampering in and out of the woods which, in spring, were covered in bluebells. Quite enough to amuse and interest us.

There were no tractors in those days so ploughing was done with horses displaying their splendid brasses on their harness. Wagons and carts were horse drawn. These horses were wonderful creatures, generally known as 'shire' horses, of which there were many different breeds. Nowadays few remain, except for those kept by enthusiasts who like to keep some of these breeds to avoid them disappearing totally.

My grandfather's farm also boasted a cart horse named 'Captain', which we loved to feed with hay and apples. Haymaking was always a joyous occasion, but wily old Captain generally managed to go lame when there was work to do. Apples and plums were picked in season, packed and sent for sale to Covent Garden fruit market in the City. Chickens were free range on the farm, but there were hen houses from where most of the eggs were collected. These were packed in special boxes to avoid breakages and sent by train to the London markets. Broody hens were shut up into a special hut and it was always a delight to see the little chicks when hatched.

I always enjoyed 'helping' old Williams prepare the feed for the pigs. It consisted of a mash with household scraps stirred in.

The Breach, Cranbrook, Kent

After milking Daisy, the family Jersey cow, Williams would bring the milk up from the farm to the house in two buckets, each dangling from either side of a yoke over his shoulder. The milk would be left in the milk parlour next to the kitchen, part to be used for the house and the remainder poured into a large bowl for the cream to settle to come to the surface. The cream was then skimmed off whilst the skimmed milk residue was fed to the calves. As soon as there was sufficient cream available we would watch Williams pour it into a churn, then, turning the churn handle until magically butter was formed. Excess butter was sold locally.

Opposite the house was a large lawn with a tennis court and a croquet lawn. There was also a superb bed of different coloured rhododendrons in the centre beyond the tennis court. It was a magnificent sight when in flower. Nearby was the 'wilderness', an area surrounded by hedges reserved for the children, in which there was a swing as well as plots for us to experiment with a little gardening. Beside the house there was a big cedar tree which tended to make some of the rooms a little dark. In summer afternoon tea was often served in the shade of this tree. Nearby there was an even bigger cedar, which must have been very old. Not far from the house on another farm there was a rookery in the trees with hundreds of squawking birds. They would fly off during the day to forage for food and return squawking to their nests as dusk fell. A walled kitchen garden produced vegetables, peaches and pears for the house according to season.

If we were staying at the Breach at the same time as my grandparents, Kate and the maids would also be there. When the grandparents were not in residence we brought our own staff. Buttered bread with early morning tea was brought to our rooms, followed by hot water for the wash basins. In those days too we used chamber pots. There was also a bathroom, and two lavatories, one upstairs and one downstairs, always much in demand. There was no electricity so we were lit by oil lamps, and went up to bed with our lighted candles in candlesticks. We were all very fond of a particular candlestick in the small bedroom. It was a china dress with the inscription

'Little Miss Etticoat,
In A White Petticoat
With A Red Nose:
The Longer She Stands,
The Shorter She Grows'

as the candle burned down. We all wanted to inherit it but quite rightly Biddy got it and has since passed it on to her son Gyles.

Eventually a petrol-driven motor was installed in one of the outhouses. It drove a dynamo which fed a series of lead batteries to give electric light to the house. I took great interest in watching progress as the place was prepared and the machinery and batteries installed. Collard was taught to operate the system. Constant testing of the acid in the batteries was required to maintain them in good order, by pouring in distilled water from large glass jars. Some years later, of course, the local electricity company took over to replace the installation.

Before my time grandfather held shooting parties at the Breach. In those days there was quite a lot of game which became gradually very scarce as the surrounding larger estates were sold or broken up. However I do recall a magnificent Golden cock pheasant in its cage on the lawn in front of the house.

Grandfather was almost a pioneer motorist. He bought his first car in 1905, an 8 H.P. Single cylinder Darracq, which was followed in 1906 by a 10 H.P. 2 cylinder Darracq and subsequent different cars. He was fond of driving to his farm in Kent. I never knew him as a driver as he gave up long before I came on the scene. My grandmother became the family driver and carried on till she was not only quite old but also rather a public danger. When she finally gave up a chauffeur was engaged but he did not turn out to be very satisfactory.

In pre-1914 days family businesses were not taxed so heavily, so my grandfather became quite comfortably well off, able to send his children to good schools, his sons to The Abbey preparatory school in Beckenham and to Tonbridge School, a well-known public school in Kent. I do not know where my aunts Agnes and Bernice were educated.

Although I never knew my aunt Agnes, she was apparently a very fine pianist, taught by one of the great teachers in London at that time, Francesco Berger. She was destined to become a concert pianist but unfortunately died of peritonitis at the age of eighteen. She is also reputed to have had a magnetic personality, loved and admired by all who came into contact with her.

Both my father and aunt Bernice were also very musical. My father was considered to have been a good violinist. He used to play, accompanied by my mother or by his sister Bernice, at the piano in the earlier days of my life but he gave

Grandfather's second Darracq car, 1906

it up later. My grandfather was also a music lover, although I do not remember him ever having played an instrument. In the nineteen thirties when radio-gramophones came into their own, he became a fanatical collector of gramophone records, buying and cataloguing practically every classical gramophone record produced: cases and cases of them, which I do not believe he played more than once.

He was generous to his family and close friends. He had bought a Steinway baby grand piano which aunt Bernice acquired after aunt Agnes died. He also bought a Steinway as a wedding present for my mother. There were also Bechstein pianos at both his houses in Beckenham and Cranbrook. He was an avid collector of paintings, which he bought from young artists selling their canvases at Smithfield. It was hardly possible to see any spare wall space at Hillside, my grandparent's house in Beckenham, on account of these pictures. Most were sold after his death, aged eighty, during the 1939-45 war. I was overseas in the army at that time but I believe some of the artists were well known. He also bought houses for aunt Bernice when she married Cecil Hayne and for uncle Douglas when his estate agency business failed. In addition he was generous in support of some of his less well off relations, and helped various characters he met in the Markets at Smithfield.

Apart from our family of four, my uncle 'Tig' and aunt Winnie had two children — my cousins Audrey and Christopher. Uncle George and aunt Marjorie had a son and two daughters, my cousins, John, Jane and Jill. Aunt Bernice and uncle Cecil Hayne had a son and three daughters, William, Margaret (Noggs), Jeanette (Nicky) and Tilly. Uncle Douglas had no children of his own. He married Lilian, the widow of his best friend, Reginald Follit, a pilot in the First World War who was shot down and killed. Reginald and Lilian had a son, Roy Follit, who thus became my step-cousin.

On the Longley side of the family, as far as I know at the time of writing, apart from my nephews and nieces, only my cousins John, Jane, Jill, William, Jeanette and Tilly are still living.

I never knew my Hovenden grandfather, who had died long before I was born, nor really did I know my grandmother as she died shortly after my birth. My mother had two elder sisters, Florence (Flo) and Charlotte (Hetty) who respectively married William and George Goodchild, farmers in Essex. Florence had eight children, four sons and four daughters, my cousins, Tom, Elizabeth, Robert, Catherine, John, William, Maria, Phoebe. Hetty had four children, one son and three daughters, Charlotte (Carly), Jim, Edith, Alice. William and Jim were killed in the 1939-45 war. As far as I know at the time of writing Maria is the only Goodchild cousin still living.

The Hovendens trace their ancestry back to the fifteenth century, after they came from Flanders to settle in the Cranbrook area of Kent. They prospered. Several of the old mansions developed from the ancient cloth halls had been owned by my ancestors.

My mother's great uncle, Robert Hovenden, compiled a book on the 'Pedigree of The Family of Hovenden' which was printed privately and distributed to all his closest relatives in 1908. The book includes a family tree and copies of Hovenden Wills, the oldest of which concerns Robert Hovenden of Cranbrook, clothier, who died in 1557. Among several pages of bequests he left ' ----*Item I geue and bequethe to my sonne Gyles Hovenden fourtie powndes to be payde to the sayde Gyles when he cometh to the age of xx yeres. ---*'

From clothiers, and cordwainers, my mother's side of the family became perfumers in the business of Robert Hovenden and Sons, which eventually became a very prosperous business, supplying hairdressers with all their needs, including the fitting out and furnishing of hairdressing salons. My maternal grandfather and his brothers were partners in the business. He spent some time in Paris prior to his marriage to my grandmother in 1886. I understand his role was to keep an eye on the perfume market in France and to purchase the essential oils needed for the family business to produce its own perfumes, hair tonics, etcetera. He died of cancer and left his daughters sufficient capital for them to enjoy a very respectable private income.

In supplying and outfitting barber's shops and hairdressers, the Hovendens naturally became members of the Worshipful Company of Barber-Surgeons, one of the many City of London Guilds. Barbers in old times were the original surgeons. In the Barbers' Hall in London there is a Holbein painting depicting King Henry VIII presenting the Barbers with their Company Charter. Several Hovendens became Masters of the Barbers including my grandfather Hovenden.

Later my brother Charles was proposed and accepted to become a Freeman of the City of London which entitled him to be elected a member of the Barbers. He then went on to become a Liveryman of the Company, was elected to the Court and finally Master. It is from being a Freeman of the City of London one can apply to become an Alderman and then a Sheriff of the City of London. It is from the ranks of Sheriffs that the Lord Mayor of London is elected. Becoming an Alderman and a Sheriff is very costly, whilst Lord Mayors have to be very wealthy indeed to aspire to their one year of office. Livery companies do not today generally play an active part in the professions from which they arose but are invariably trustees of charities, private schools and other worthy causes. The Barbers specialise in charities connected with the medical profession. Many of its members are doctors and surgeons, including several well-known professors at the London teaching hospitals. My brother Charles was an active member on the various charitable committees and much enjoyed this voluntary work.

The Hovenden business finally ceased to exist in the late nineteen thirties.

Early Years (1918 -1932)

We were a happy family of four. My elder brother, Charles, was nearly four years older. My sister, Biddy, is just over a year younger than I. Dennis was five years younger.

Charles died in his 93rd year in 2008 and Dennis aged 84 in 2009. Biddy celebrated her 90th birthday with her family in Scotland in December 2009.

The differences in the ages between my brothers and me was such that in our childhood and adolescent years, although we knew each other well and did things together as a family, our interests and friends were different. However we got on well together and I do not remember much jealousy between us. Apart from a term together at our prep school with my elder brother none of us were at school together. As a child therefore I was not very close to my brothers, nor all that much with my sister, as girls were not of great interest to boys at that age.

Later of course when we were grown up, and especially after the war, and all married, we became increasingly closer and much enjoyed each others' company.

My parents were very loving towards us and did not display any favouritism. My mother told me that she had hoped for a girl and instead got me. There is no doubt when my sister was born my parents were overjoyed and I suspect Biddy received special attention on account of this. Whilst I may have had bouts of jealousy at times they were only temporary and never a real problem. However over the years I did come to realise that I did not have the advantage of being the oldest child, nor the only daughter, nor the youngest child. As this situation gradually dawned on me I believe that it played an important role in the development of my character. There were later to be other good reasons why this should be.

Like my mother I am left handed. I do not think efforts were made to correct this but I have always had difficulty to write well. At school we learned to write in ink with steel pen nibs. It always annoyed me that school desks were made for right handed pupils with the ink pot on the wrong side as far as I was concerned. I played tennis, squash and fives and did most things left handed, but I batted right hand at cricket.

My parents were comfortably well off so that whilst we did not live extravagantly we lived well but were not spoilt.

Both our parents were quite tolerant towards us. Although they must have been frustrated by the antics and behaviour of their offspring at times they seldom expressed anger, but rather disappointment. A look of disapproval was often sufficient to bring us to order.

Both my parents were heavy smokers. My father smoked Wills Gold Flake cigarettes whilst my mother was addicted to Mr Rothman's cigarettes. She would order them from Rothmans of Pall Mall by the thousand at a time, ten tin boxes of 100. Thus throughout our childhood and adult lives we were subjected to intensive secondary smoking. There was a constant blue haze of smoke in the lounge. Ever since I can remember my mother had a very pronounced smoker's cough. This cough always embarrassed and irritated me. I never got used to it.

As adults, we all — my brothers, sister and I — became smokers. Despite all this smoke my elder brother lived to 93 and my younger brother to 84 whilst Biddy and I are into our nineties. I do not wish to draw any morals from this, nor advocate smoking. We all eventually gave up smoking and are no longer able to bear other people's smoke.

Mother made good use of Rothmans cigarette gift coupons which were exchanged for many useful items, one of which

My sister and I

was our first commercially produced, battery operated, wireless set, in about 1928. Hitherto we had been forced to put up with my father's home-made wireless sets, with all their various valves and dials.

There was a moment when mother adopted another brand of cigarette, which had a better gift catalogue. Her desertion soon brought a letter from Mr Sidney Rothman himself expressing his disappointment at losing such a valuable customer. Mother promptly returned to Rothmans and remained faithful thereafter.

My earliest recollections were at 44 Manor Road, crawling around on the lawn in summer with my sister Biddy, feeding our rabbits, and making mud pies.

Never to be forgotten were the appalling pea soup fogs which were quite prevalent in those days. For anyone today, after the Clean Air Act prohibited the use of coal fires, it would be an unbelievable experience. These fogs sometimes lasted several days. Our house was near a cross roads. The local council set up flares on the street corners to guide the traffic. It was not until some years later that traffic lights were introduced at this cross roads. We could also hear the loud bangs on the railways which warned the train drivers about signals which of course they could not see in the fog.

At this time the streets were lit by gas lamps. A lamplighter would cycle with his special long pole to switch on the gas which was then ignited from a pilot lamp. Electric street lights were gradually introduced later.

The local cinema, known as the 'flea pit', showed the usual silent films of the time. The programme started with a shorter feature, generally known as a 'B' film, followed by an interval. The main film was often a cowboy film, during which a pianist in the pit would play appropriate music to accompany the action. Later a new posh cinema, 'The Regal', with a restaurant, was built. This much more modern and comfortable place became the central attraction of the town. At first, there was a piano player to accompany the films until the talking films gradually took over from the silent ones.

With our Nannie

Much to my delight, a Wurlitzer organ was installed. The organist played during the interval; the impressive instrument would gradually rise from the pit until in full view at the front of the stage. Wurlitzer organs were a must for all respectable cinemas, some of their organists, such as Reginald Dickson, becoming very well known. I always enjoyed the recital during the interval and much admired the showmanship of the organist. They would play both classical and popular pieces.

Chocolates and ice creams would be readily available from the uniformed usherettes. And, of course, smoking was permitted in the auditorium. For a family outing we would sometimes have tea in the restaurant before or after the performance.

When we were a little older we would often be taken to see a play at the Penge Empire, the local theatre, at the nearby town of that name. Many towns had theatres and some good thrillers or comedies were performed by well known theatrical companies.

Another feature of those days were the popular Lyons teashops, where you were served by the famous Lyons 'Nippy' waitresses. Pre-war Lyons was a big business supplying Lyons brands of tea, ice creams, and cup cakes. They also ran the Lyons Corner Houses in London, which had reasonably good restaurants and sold take-away food. They also owned the rather more up-market Trocadero restaurant at Piccadilly, quite a favourite of my parents, who took us there from time to time. There were luscious displays of hors d'oeuvres. My mother always took Turkish coffee which was served by a Turk, or at least a man dressed as such. He would offer some rose water to put into the coffee and to our delight would sprinkle some on to our hands.

Right from a very early age we attended the morning service at Christ Church, Beckenham, where we occupied the family pew reserved for my grandparents, my family and any other members of the family, uncles, aunts and cousins who might be attending as well.

For a long time I was fascinated by a notice posted on the pillars of the church which said 'All seats free after the organ starts'. I wondered how much they cost before the organ started. It took me a long time to realise it meant reserved pews became free to sit in if they are not occupied when the organ starts.

We had a family dog, Bobby, often referred to as Heinz, on account of his many varieties, part Jack Russell, part Sealyham, part Corgi, with other ingredients involved in his creation. Bobby was a character well known in the town, as he often wandered off, getting separated from the family. He had the reputation of taking the No 109 bus on his own to come back home. In fact it is said the bus conductors knew where to stop the bus to let him get off. There was also a large ginger cat called Fluffy we all loved dearly.

My elder brother was a model railway buff so an upper room on the second floor was made into the 'train room', where my father and brother set up lines for the electric model trains. These worked off the main electric plug so when you received an electric shock you did not touch the plug or lines a second time. More refined systems were later installed with transformers which reduced the risk.

In those days the Walls ice cream man with his tricycle patrolled the streets and would call if a 'W' Walls sign was placed in the front room window. He had many different kinds of ices in his box, ranging from a simple water ice up to ice cakes.

There was also a 'CP' sign which was displayed to attract Carter Paterson, the carriers, principally to send clothes to be cleaned by Pullars of Perth. There were no local cleaners, or if there were, they were not considered as good as Pullars. The goods were returned in boxes bound by string. Whilst my mother was inclined to be a bit extravagant, she was quite the opposite for certain things, such as unravelling the strings into little balls which were carefully stowed away for future use, wasting a considerable amount of drawer space.

She did the same with the protecting tissue paper in which the clothes were packed, neatly folding them.

Whilst at Manor Road my brother went to Clare House preparatory school in Beckenham. Later, for health reasons, he went to Streete Court School at Westgate-on-Sea in the Isle of Thanet, Kent.

My first school was Miss Woodham's school in Beckenham. I met my friend John Morris there. I was always a fairly shy person as a child and not very given to conversation. My family always teased me about my friendship with John. We would take it in turns to visit each others' houses. 'Good morning, John' —'Good morning, Gyles' — we would greet each other before getting down to the serious matter of playing with our toys. Almost without a further word we would part company —'Goodbye, Gyles' — 'Goodbye, John', going on our separate ways. Presence to me has always been more important than chatter.

Although I can remember the faces of some of the teachers and pupils, I do not remember their names, other than Miss Aste who taught me bible stories. There was a rather pretty girl who was a member of the Robertson marmalade family, and my friend John.

It is not easy now for me to recall childhood memories with great accuracy. In addition to the Breach our holidays were spent either at various seaside resorts such as Bexhill on Sea and Weymouth. We enjoyed playing on the sands, shrimping, or getting up early in the morning — depending on the tide — to catch prawns under the rocks. We ate ice cream cornets from the barrows of Italian ice cream vendors, and very enjoyable buns and cakes after a swim. Generally we stayed in hotels but sometimes in guest houses.

Concert party shows on the piers, not forgetting the inevitable Punch-and-Judy shows were a great treat, as were paddle steamer trips from and to various seaside piers. I always spent much of my time on the paddle steamers fascinated, watching the pistons driving the paddles. The smell of the oily steam was like nectar to me.

My brothers and sister, 1926

The first car I remember in the family was an open tourer Cubitt which took us to Devon and Cornwall. It was eventually changed for a saloon Cubitt. After the Cubitts I do not think we had another car for a number of years, instead father hired a Godfrey Davis hire car for holidays.

We often went to London by train from Beckenham junction, generally with my mother, for a shopping spree. We would travel by steam train to Victoria station. To do so the train had to go through the Penge tunnel. Whoever was nearest the carriage window quickly pulled on the window strap to shut out the engine smoke. To get to and from Beckenham station a horse drawn cab was summoned. One never forgets those familiar smells of horses and steam trains. Alas, the horse cabs were gradually replaced by taxis and steam by electric trains. Ever a traditionalist, mother always took a cab until the last cabby retired.

Beckenham Junction had an extensive coal siding where large deposits of coal were stored under the names of the various coal merchants supplying coal and coke for domestic household needs. These firms had their local offices outside the station. Coal was delivered in sacks by horse drawn carts. Every house possessed a coal hole cover on the pavement outside. The coalmen would heave a heavy sack onto their backs, remove the coal hole cover, then pour the contents down into the cellars. Anthracite, the most satisfactory type of coal for the house coal fires, went down the coal hole whilst the lighter coke fuel for the heating and greenhouse boilers was delivered directly to wherever it was required.

We had a large settee in our lounge with six square cushions. I played for hours pretending to be a coalman setting up his sacks vertically on the settee to haul them onto my back to pour down a mythical coal hole, then fold the empty sacks like a true coalman.

As a family we would sometimes travel to Scotland by the *Flying Scotsman* on the London and North Eastern Railway (L.N.E.R.) line up to Edinburgh on the eastern side of the country. Railway engines with their beautiful movement of pistons, driving rods and wheels always fascinated both men and boys. In order to travel non-stop to Edinburgh the engine scooped up water from water troughs at various stages along the journey. Delicious meals would be served and one marvelled how the stewards were able to balance plates on their trays as the train swayed. In those days British trains were the fastest in the world.

My brother Dennis was born at Manor Road in 1923. We had a nurse, Nannie, who first came to look after my sister Biddy and me. She had to leave in 1926 as she became pregnant. She subsequently married the father of her child and they had a very happy life together.

Another nurse did not last long. She was followed in 1927 by Ellen Alexander Coath, who was successively styled as Miss Coath, 'Couchie' or 'Nell'. Nell Coath came to look after Dennis as his governess, and stayed with my family to become housekeeper, and finally, until her retirement, companion to my mother. She was a very competent person adored by all the family, a great influence for the good of us all. She never married. She also added to the family habit of smoking, helping to thicken those blue smoke clouds around the house.

Around this time we moved to another larger house in Beckenham — Chelston, in Overbury Avenue. It had three floors: a ground floor, over an extensive group of cellars, and two upper floors. The ground floor had a spacious hall leading into the lounge, the dining room, and the morning room, which we used for various activities. Behind the swinging green baize door, separating the family area from the servants' quarters, there was a large kitchen with a coal fire kitchen range, a scullery, various pantries, toilets, etcetera. The first floor included my parents' room, Charles' room, Biddy's room and a room which Dennis and I shared. The second consisted of Nell Coath's room, the maids' room, Dennis' nursery and the inevitable 'train room'.

We also had a much larger garden with a very competent gardener whom we took over from the previous owners of the house. The garden was in three parts with the tennis lawn at the rear of the house surrounded by well tended flower beds, next was a lawn mown orchard with apples, pears, and plum trees with flower beds around each tree. The third section had a croquet lawn, a herbaceous border and a kitchen garden producing much of the family's vegetable and fruit requirements. There was also a separate garage. Our gardener's name was Taylor, generally referred to as 'old Taylor'. Practically no plants were bought, most being cultivated from seed, or cuttings, which were brought to bedding out condition in a large greenhouse. There was also a conservatory adjoining the lounge where Taylor grew magnificent displays of chrysanthemums, gloxinia and other appropriate plants according to the season. Many cups for chrysanthemums, sweet peas, and vegetables were won at local flower shows.

Taylor's wife, compared to her husband, was a fairly powerful woman. She handled the family laundry which was done in an outhouse across the yard from the kitchen. Sheets, towels, and clothes were boiled in a boiler and mangled on a hand-operated mangle. This arrangement was quite satisfactory until Taylor had a child with the cook. Mrs Taylor left us; so did the cook, who set up home with the gardener.

Shortly after this episode a very persuasive salesman sold the family a Canadian made electric washing machine complete with automatic mangler. It was a much more complicated affair with several tubs compared with a modern machine. It never broke down and served the family well until the forties or fifties. There was also an electric roller iron on which all the sheets, towels, table cloths were dealt with.

In 1926 the General Strike paralysed all activity for nine days. It started with the miners and spread throughout the country, almost causing a revolution. I well remember my family's concern, particularly on account of the transport of meat and other perishable products.

Boarding School (1928 - 1935)

In 1928, at the age of ten, I went to my first boarding school — Streete Court preparatory school, at Westgate-on-Sea — to join my brother Charles for a term or two, before he went off to Tonbridge School. It was a good school and I enjoyed my time there. The headmaster was a Mr Longrigg, the second master Mr Deakin, and a very helpful master Mr Peebles, among others. I was always very home-sick when my parents took me up to Victoria station. There was a special train which took us, as well as other children going to other schools on the line, to Birchington, Broadstairs, Margate and other seaside towns in the area.

The journey to Westgate was sixty miles through the East Kent countryside. I well remember the large billboards which advertised 'Carters Little Liver Pills' every mile, each indicating how many miles from London. There were also 'Halls Distemper' billboards depicting two painters supporting a ladder and each of them carrying a pot of Halls distemper. These advertising boards were more elegant than the rather blatant advertising of today.

During the week we wore grey flannel shorts and a jacket, but on Sundays and special occasions, like half term visits by our parents, we wore the official school uniform of a particular dark cloth only purchasable at Gooch's, or other authorised outfitters, in London. We also wore stiff Eton collars and bowler hats. A strange sight we must have been, as we walked to the local church on Sundays, dressed in this garb.

We all came to school with our 'tuck' boxes, a sort of wooden trunk, which contained our clothing and other accessories as well as our 'tuck' consisting of chocolates and sweets. The latter were immediately confiscated on arrival and issued out to us in very small quantities by the headmaster's wife after lunch on Sundays.

We also had to hand over any money, which was duly registered. We were able to use this money for any purchases which the headmaster's wife would procure for us, providing our requirements were considered suitable. Thanks to the odd tip from visiting relatives I always managed to return home with more money than I started with. Even in those days I lived within my income.

I think I was about average scholastically, doing rather well in Latin but not so well in Mathematics. I loved Geography and History but was not very good at playing cricket nor rugby which were the main sports. However the School held its own very well against competition from other schools in the area. I remember one outstanding cricketer, D. G. Clark, a son of the founder of the famous Foster Clark custard cream company. He went on to captain Kent, and was President of the M.C.C. in 1977-78.

I made many friends at Streete Court, some of whom came from well known families. There was a Waley-Cohen, whose father was a famous World War I veteran who had lost both his legs in the war. He was always in a wheelchair but that did not prevent him from being a very active Jewish member of parliament. G. A. Singer, always known as Gas, came from the family of the American Singer Sewing Machine Company. There was a Gibson whose father's contracting company had built one of the early Aswam dams in the Sudan. Many also came from Yorkshire whose families were owners of cloth mills.

Although I never became a sailor, it was during my time at this school that I became aware of my love for ships. They fascinated me, so I devoured books and articles on all kinds of ships, particularly the annual editions of Jane's Fighting Ships, to keep me abreast of details of the latest ships in the Fleet. As I was interested in the Royal Navy I joined the Navy

League which was a sort of friends of the Navy organisation. With my family we visited the naval dockyards at Chatham when they were open to the public on Navy Day. I was thrilled to scramble over battleships, submarines and other vessels. I acquired a book on Dartmouth Naval College and thought I would like to join the navy eventually. I was, however, a little disappointed to note that an admiral did not earn as much as I would have liked. I have never to this day ceased to be interested in ships and the sea. My mother also had this great love of ships.

Another imaginary hobby of mine was archaeology, which I picked up from copies of the *Illustrated London News* which frequently had news and illustrations of archaeological findings in various parts of the world. This paper, together with *Country Life* and similar magazines, were provided for us to read on Sunday afternoons. Although I never indulged in any archaeological work the fascination for silent cities and ancient stones has remained with me throughout my life.

For my birthday I had been given a hand-operated Pathé 8mm film projector and took this with me to school. As I was the only boy to own one I gave 'cinema' shows. The films were quite short, mostly — 'Felix the Cat', Charlie Chaplin, Harold Lloyd — as well as some ghastly horror features. Later I was able to update the equipment by adding a motor and other extensions to enable much longer film reels to be shown.

Charles was given a Pathé 8 mm movie camera to enable him to record family scenes. One brother having the projector and the other the camera did sometimes cause problems when each wanted to use the projector for his own films.

Over the years we built up a very full library of films taken of the family as we grew up from childhood, married, and brothers and sister in their turn had children. When we were all together we had great fun in re-running these old family films.

Dennis finally became the family custodian of the equipment, camera, projector and films. When it became possible to re-record these old films on to digital discs, Dennis had the ambition to do this with our films but unfortunately died before he was able to do so.

Streete Court was in a lovely setting of woodland in the otherwise flat open grain growing country of the Isle of Thanet. Nearby was Manston R.A.F. Airdrome, always fascinating to us boys. School walks would take us to Quex Park, the private natural history museum of a well known big game hunter. He had created a wonderful display of stuffed wild animals, elephants, giraffes, tigers and many others set in typical surroundings.

My parents would come down to Westgate to take me out each day of the half term period. They would stay with Robert Hovenden, a second cousin of my mother, who had a splendid house just down the road from the school. 'Uncle Bob', now elderly, was the last owner of the Robert Hovenden and Sons firm. He was very rich, had a beautiful garden — with many greenhouses, producing his own fruit and vegetables — a housekeeper, butler, cook, housemaids, and a chauffeur, 'Rowley', to drive the Daimler car. His pride was his immaculate croquet lawn. He had a sister, Margaret, who was often there, but lived in London and was a member of Roehampton, the equivalent of the M.C.C., for croquet. They often had arguments about the rules of croquet.

Uncle Bob was a local Justice of the Peace and well known character. Meals there were always excellent, with a butler in attendance. My parents much appreciated his excellent wine cellar.

One room of the house always fascinated me. It was his museum, with a collection of various artefacts from World War I as well as a telescope from which one could watch the ships passing up the Thames estuary. We could also see the Goodwin Sands on which many vessels had been ensnared over the centuries. A World War I bomb shelter in the garden was forbidden territory, as it was considered unsafe. During that war there was, not far from the house, a seaplane base which was bombed from time to time.

Uncle Bob died, about 1936, leaving over £250,000 — which was quite a fortune in those days. I believe my mother got 'a little something' from the estate but the bulk of it went to various charities and to his nephew.

Many pupils at Street Court gained scholarships at well known public schools such as Wellington, Uppingham, Marlborough, Stowe and others, but I do not recall any for Tonbridge. However I was not in the class of scholarship but managed to pass my common entrance into Tonbridge, which was by anyone's standards a very well known 'Public School' in Kent.

The Great Depression started in America in 1929 which affected the whole world and inevitably had its repercussions on all businesses, including those of my family. People ate less meat so all this affected the family's finances. Some economies had to be made, so for many years we did not own a car but still managed to keep a gardener, cook and housemaid in addition to Nell.

Over the years it became increasingly difficult to find good staff as young people were no longer willing to enter domestic service. We were lucky and had some very good cooks and housemaids but they soon left to marry and found families. Many of them remained true family friends and came to visit us from time to time.

The depression went on for several years until Roosevelt introduced his New Deal. But economies really only began to pick up when countries started to re-arm to counterbalance the growing threat to peace from Hitler's Germany. By the time I left Streete Court I was becoming aware that Britain, France and many other countries were concerned about the rise of this German personage.

Tonbridge School (1932 - 1935)

Although I did not realise the full significance of the problems of those days it was in this context that, at the age of thirteen in 1932, I thus followed the family tradition and went as a boarder to Judde House, Tonbridge School. My brother Charles had left the term before I arrived.

Tonbridge School, according to the School website, was founded in 1553 by Sir Andrew Judd, under Letters Patent of King Edward VI. The Charter ordained that the Governors of the school after the death of the Founder were to be the Worshipful Company of Skinners, one of the oldest City Livery Companies. Sir Andrew, himself a distinguished member of this Company, left property in the City of London and in the parish of St Pancras as an endowment for the school. The income from these estates is at the disposal of the Governors for the general benefit of the School. The memory of Sir Andrew Judd and other benefactors is honoured in an annual Commemoration Service, held on Skinners' Day at the end of the Summer Term.

William Owen Chadwick was Head of School much of my time. He later became a well known history professor, writer and prominent Christian historian, and is one of the few people awarded an O.M. (Order of Merit) as well as K.B.E.

There must have been a fair shortage of qualified teachers in those days due to the effects of the First World War. Many were fairly elderly and some had served in the armed forces and had been injured.

One of my maths teachers was deaf and had a primitive hearing aid attached to a sort of microphone which he constantly tapped to see if it was working properly. I am afraid we used to make fun of him by pretending there was a bee buzzing in the class room to cause him to tap his instrument. However, although I never had much competence at mathematics, it would be unfair to lay the blame on this kindly master.

Another had lost his arm so had a metallic artificial arm and hand. He was nick-named 'Tinfin' and taught us science which was a subject which did interest me. On the whole they, and all the masters, some with their particular oddities, were excellent. Despite their valiant efforts they did not succeed in turning me into a brilliant scholar. My preferred subjects were more into science, especially chemistry and biology. Gradually these interests led me to consider aiming for a medical career.

Tonbridge had not only a fine scholastic record; it was also remarkable in the field of sports. Our cricket and rugby teams more often than not used to beat Eton, Harrow, and many other famous schools. We were one of the top schools for racquets, athletics, rifle shooting, amongst other sports. I was not a worthy cricketer, nor rugbyman, but enjoyed playing hockey, squash, fives and running, playing these sports with adequate enthusiasm but without distinction.

I was confirmed into the Anglican faith at the lovely Tonbridge School chapel, where my father and his brothers had worshipped. The Confirmation service was taken by the Bishop of Rochester. The occasion has remained a milestone in my life. Chapel played a very large part in my life at school. There was a short morning service before lessons and prayers at the end of the day. A full morning service was held on Sundays as well as a full Evensong. For those concerned there was a Holy Communion service before breakfast but this was voluntary as opposed to the other services which were compulsory.

I always enjoyed the pre-breakfast walk for Communion from Judde House to the Chapel with the prospect of a grilled sausage, only one, for breakfast on my return. Meals at school were perhaps not wonderful but we survived nevertheless. That being said I have never, at least since World War II, tasted such nice spicy sausages as in those days. I also enjoyed evening supper after chapel on Sundays when we would have a boiled egg, the only one of the week. However we could always supplement our meals with fried eggs or baked beans on toast at the school 'grubber'.

We were six in the 'novi' intake at Judde House when I joined the school in the winter term of 1932. Two of them subsequently died in World War II. My best friend, David Wingate, a pilot, was killed in the Battle of Britain in 1940. Another of my good friends, Robert Hobbs, who followed into his family business of estate agents and auctioneers in Ashford, Kent, was to die relatively young some years after the war. Spending much of my life overseas shortly after leaving Tonbridge I lost contact, with a few exceptions, with most of my school contemporaries.

These included my step-cousin, Roy Follit, who was a little older and senior to me. He was a boarder at Park House. Whilst we saw much of each other at school it was only after we had both left that we became inseparable friends and enjoyed our early adult life together. We both played hockey for teams at the Beckenham Hockey club, also squash and tennis, dances and the inevitable pub crawls. We also went on two cruises in the Mediterranean before the war. Roy married Joan Brothers in 1939 and had a daughter, Pera, who became my goddaughter.

At the outbreak of war Roy joined the Queen's Own Royal West Kent Regiment (QORWK). I was to follow Roy when I joined the 5th Battalion QORWK on my commission in 1941. Although I did not know it, he was killed at Salerno on the 16th September 1943 whilst fighting with the 4th Hampshire Regiment, not far from my own position on the battlefield at the time.

Although I enjoyed my school years I was by no means a scholar nor a competent athlete or sportsman. I think I can confidently say I was below average.

In fact I left Tonbridge School in 1935 having failed to pass the School Certificate exam. This of course was a considerable disappointment for my parents. The School Certificate enabled one to apply for a place at university, which was necessary for me to pursue my ambition to train to become a doctor of medicine, an ambition I had been nurturing for some time.

Accordingly I went to a crammer in London, Marcy's in Chancery Lane. I was joined by a fellow Old Tonbridgian, Alan Collins, who had also failed his School certificate. We both succeeded in passing the London Matriculation, equivalent to the School certificate. I was therefore qualified to apply to for a place at one of the London Teaching Hospitals.

As I was about to apply for a place at the Middlesex Hospital Medical School I had second thoughts, feeling I was not really cut out for a medical career. Furthermore I felt I was not sufficiently keen to rely on my parents having to support me during several years of training. No doubt too the general international situation was a contributing factor to an unsettling period of my life. Understandably my parents were not at all happy about my decision.

I was then faced with the problem of what career to follow, particularly as I had no qualifications nor particular skills. My parents suggested I should go for a consultation at The British Institute of Industrial Psychology to find out their opinion on what sort of job or career for which I might be suited. I underwent several written, visual, oral and practical tests at their centre in London, which resulted in a report which suggested I was suitable for employment in an electricity showroom or similar. This was rather a blow to my pride so I quietly said to myself 'to Hell with that'.

Although I did not realise it at the time this was a turning point in my life when, shortly afterwards, I ceased to be dependent on my family and started to earn my own living.

I worked for a little while in the office of my father's business in Smithfield, with one of the clerks who gave me enormous columns of figures in ledgers to add up. Whilst he could add these up in a flash, they would take me some time and then the result was generally incorrect. Decidedly, arithmetic was not my strong point, but in later life figures played an important part in my career.

While I was passing the time wondering what to do, and out of favour with my father and mother, our housekeeper and governess, Nell Coath, spotted an advertisement in the Times newspaper and suggested I should apply for the job.

I duly did.

Gestetner (1936)

My letter received an immediate reply from a firm called Gestetner. I was invited to London to meet the Office Manager, at the Gestetner British Sales Organisation (BSO), in Aldwych House in the Strand on the following Monday.

This being my first and only application for a job, I was most surprised to be asked to start work with them the next week as a clerk in the BSO's London office. With a view to future expansion the firm was seeking to recruit young public or grammar school boys to train them for future positions in the company, either on the sales or administrative sides of the business. Despite my lack of qualifications this was apparently sufficient. In those days you learned on the job. I do not remember my starting salary but do not think it was more than five shillings a week.

On the evening of 30th November 1936, the day before I joined Gestetner, the Crystal Palace caught fire and burned down. Sydenham Hill is not far from where we lived at Beckenham. It was a fantastic blaze visible for miles around. In fact the night sky was so brightly lit it could be seen as far away as Essex, north-east of London. We rushed to the scene in the family car, which by then was a Morris. Thousands came from all around but we were naturally barred from getting too close by a police cordon. Even our cousins from Essex came to view the scene.

The Crystal Palace, originally in Hyde Park, was a lattice of cheap cast iron and plate glass designed by Joseph Paxton and built in 1851 to house the *Great Exhibition of the Works of Industry of all Nations,* a British response to the French Industrial Exposition of 1844. After the exhibition, the building was dismantled and moved to Penge Common, which became the Crystal Palace Park.

It was for us a sad ending to this great building, which had stood there for 82 years. As a family we were often taken to the Crystal Palace to have dinner and watch the splendid firework displays frequently held there. There was also a speedway dirt track in the grounds, among other attractions. We loved to watch the races when some famous riders were taking part. One of my favourite riders was Roger Frogley, the first British Star Rider, who retired when the track closed in 1932, and is almost completely forgotten today.

1936 was the year when Britain had three kings. On the death of George V, his son Edward VIII succeeded, but shortly afterwards abdicated in favour of his brother George VI. Hitler broke the Treaty of Versailles and occupied the Rhineland. The Spanish Civil War started. The Popular Front gained the French elections and Hitler was disgusted to watch a black competitor, Jesse Owens, win a race at the Berlin Olympics.

1936 was also the year in which I obtained my driving licence. My father was my instructor. One first obtained a provisional licence to enable one to be taught, providing the car displayed an 'L' (learner) plate or disk.

After the excitement of the Crystal Palace fire I thus took up my first and only job the following day.

I quickly discovered Gestetner was an important business manufacturing stencil duplicators and their supplies. They were manufactured at their vast factory at Tottenham in North London, and were sold throughout the world. These goods were marketed through wholly owned subsidiaries in many foreign and commonwealth countries.

The founder of the business, David Gestetner, was born in 1854 in Csorna, Hungary. At the age of seventeen, he moved to Vienna and was apprenticed to a stockbroker, where his work included making multiple hand-written copies of the day's market activity. After the fall of the Vienna stock exchange, amid the great financial crisis of 1873, he worked first with his family who had set up a restaurant in the city. In the same year he emigrated to the U.S.A. — with the proceeds, the story has it, from some of his mother's jewellery, pawned on his behalf by a fond parent. Unfortunately, soon after his arrival, his pocket was picked and he lost all his money.

Granted a loan by a charitable organisation, he found a job selling kites on the streets of Chicago. The kites were made of a light but strong Japanese paper, Yoshino paper, coated with a lacquer. David Gestetner's observant eye noted the long, strong fibres of a piece of torn kite. He returned to Vienna, and worked in partnership with an uncle making equipment for hectographs, but the business failed and in 1879 David Gestetner moved to London. It was here, fuelled by these early experiences, that his life's work on stencils began — opening up a new era of success for him and for the whole world of communications.

He took out his first patents in London in 1879 and founded his own business, the Gestetner Cyclograph Company, in 1881. In the same year he filed his patent for the *Cyclostyle*, later combining the pen with new and improved stencils, using waxed Japanese paper. Although these pens were still available when I left the Company, in the late nineteenth century they were largely replaced by typewriters for cutting stencils. In the same period, men in offices were gradually replaced by female typists. This employment of women in offices contributed greatly to their emancipation. David Gestetner not only developed cheap printing, but also indirectly played a prominent role in the leap forward of modern industrial and administrative activity to the present day.

David Gestetner was already 84 when I joined the Company, but the business was well established with a very large and complex factory in Tottenham and with branches or subsidiaries in Europe, and many other parts of the world. David had one son, Sigmund, and five daughters.

David Gestetner (1854-1939)

The Tottenham Factory, from a publicity photograph of about 1910.

The husbands of all five daughters came into the business at some time or other either in England or in Europe, as did his brothers Jacob and Arnold. Arnold's role was to develop the European businesses.

After David Gestetner retired, his son became Managing Director. Sigmund was instrumental in greatly developing the world sales organisation, employing thousands of people. The company was one of the more important companies quoted on the London Stock Exchange.

The Tottenham factory produced practically everything required for the stencil duplicating process from duplicating machines to various supplies and accessories. There was a foundry, a die-casting shop for the basic metal parts, a plastics and ceramics shop for machinery parts and other items, with an assembly shop for the machines. There was a plant for coating stencils complete with an important solvent recovery installation, a paper shop for assembling stencils, a paint shop, a shop for making inks for duplicating machines, a machine tool shop for making the tools required for all the departments. There were a number of laboratories each for a specific speciality. The Head Office was also at the factory premises at Tottenham.

I joined a team of five colleagues working in the accounts department of the BSO in Aldwych House, London. One of my new colleagues was a Swiss Italian, Mario Senti, who was the son of the manager of the Italian subsidiary. Another colourful character who kept us amused by his rather hectic night life was Pym Ormrod, brother of Roger, a young barrister who later became one of the Law Lords. Johnny Johnson, a friend of Pym's, was a dour Scotsman whose family were prominent in the Jardine Matheson business in Hong Kong. Finally there was John Cobban, a very handsome young man who charmed all the female staff. He was a keen oarsman rowing for one of the well known London clubs and a great supporter of the Everton football team.

When we were flush we would go to the Ship Inn for a roast lunch. The Ship was round the corner near Lincoln's Inn and

My Grandparents' Golden Wedding 1937:
Front row, left to right: Minnie and Oliver Longley and Aunt Bernice.
Back row, left to right: Uncles Douglas, Oliver (Tig), Charles (my
father) and George.

Left to Right, back row - Father, Grannie and Grandpa, Mother, Uncle
George and Aunt Marjorie, Uncle Will Goodchild, Aunt Winnie, Aunt
Lilian (Roy's mother). Middle row - Aunt Bernice and Uncle Cecil
Hayne, Mrs Searle (Marjorie's mother), Aunt Lig, Charles, Aunt Flo
Goodchild (Mother's sister). Front row - Christopher, Dennis, Biddy,
self, Roy Follit

to get there one had to pass Charles Dicken's 'Old Curiosity Shop' which had been well preserved since his time. When we were less flush we would buy sandwiches to eat in the office from the tea lady, ever one to pass on office gossip.

After work we would sometimes meet at the Devreux, a pub opposite the Law Courts in the Strand where we would join Pym's barrister brother. It was here we introduced our Italian friend Mario to drinking a glass of bitter. The Devreux is very near 'Temple Bar', the place of entry into the City of London. It is traditionally here where the Sovereign is obliged to seek permission from the Lord Mayor of London to enter the City. It might also be noted that the Honourable Artillery Company, my father's old regiment, is the only regiment permitted to march with fixed bayonets through the City of London.

Our work at Aldwych House was fairly humdrum, checking cash received from customers to prepare for posting onto account cards by the girls operating the Burroughs machines. These girls used to make it quite clear to us that we were rather inferior to them. We had to be careful of their sarcastic comments at times. They were particularly delighted to put us in our place if we made a mistake. We also had the task of following up customers' account queries to which we would reply by dictating to a 'dictaphone'. Our messages were recorded on wax cylinders which were then collected by the girls from the typing pool for them to type.

In the first days I did not know what the future held for me, but Sigmund Gestetner, together with one or two of his fellow directors, would wander down the office to talk to Mr R. N. Nightingale, the accounts department manager, or 'Nightie' as we all knew him. I remember overhearing Sigmund waving his hand in our direction one day casually remarking 'these boys are the future of the Company'. I was comforted by that, as I had often thought I would like to be like these well-dressed gentlemen, who so confidently strolled round the office smoking their cigarettes. Little did

Sigmund Gestetner (1897-1956)

... with the Model 66, designed by Raymond Loewy, which was in production throughout the 1930s.

I know that by successive stages I would achieve that status. It was then 1937.

About that time both Pym and Johnny entered the sales force but did not remain with the Firm for long. Mario returned to Italy to Milan to rejoin his father. John Cobban had already left to join the Continental Audit staff.

My employers seemed to appreciate my work. Towards the end of 1937 I was asked if I also would like to join the Continental Audit Staff, reporting to Head Office on the many subsidiaries the Company owned on the continent of Europe. The prospect of leaving home both frightened and attracted me. My family, however, were not keen to see their son go off to foreign countries. My grandfather was very much against it, as being a rather insular person he considered that 'wogs' started at Calais and did not want to see his grandson fall into their ways.

Finally, my inherent spirit of adventure prevailed so I accepted. Becoming a member of the Continental Audit team meant that I ceased to be a member of the BSO and became a part of the Treasury which had an office at Aldwych House but was a part of the Head Office at Tottenham. Thus I was engaged to start as a trainee auditor in January 1938 at a salary of 12 pounds a month. The Treasury came under the responsibility of Mr A. S. Bass, referred to as 'ASB', the company's director responsible for the European sales network. His right hand man in charge of the auditors was Mr E. A. Strehler, a Swiss from the German speaking part of that country. He had an office at Aldwych House.

Joining the audit team usually meant that you would eventually be offered a situation in one of the companies outside Europe. In fact I replaced another auditor, George Pitman, who had been promoted to Secretary of the South African company in Johannesburg.

European Auditing With Gestetner (1938 - 1939)

"Heil Hitler, Polizei, Passeport, bitte!"

I was to hear these words many times as I crossed the German border during my travels as a company auditor in Europe from January 1938 until the outbreak of the war on 3rd September 1939.

I was now 20 years old. We were a group of four, sometimes working together, at other times one or two of us, depending on the size of the European subsidiary. The senior member was another Swiss German, Fritz Kung, who was a friend of Gene Strehler, both being from St Gallen in Switzerland. The next senior was John Hawtry, followed by John Cobban, then me. Fritz was some years senior to the rest of us. France was our largest European subsidiary; it was only in Paris that we all met together.

Those were the days when we travelled in luxury on the great trains such as the Simplon-Orient Express, taking one to Vienna, Milan, and beyond, and the Nord Express with branches to Brussels, Amsterdam, Berlin and to Warsaw and beyond. In addition to our pay we received fairly generous expense allowances enabling us to stay in reasonably good class hotels and eat in good restaurants.

In 1938 Adolf Hitler, the German Chancellor, dominated the European — indeed the world — scene by his aggressive attitude towards Germany's neighbours. He had come to power in 1933, occupied the Sarre in the Rhineland in 1936 — thus breaking the Versailles Treaty — without any effective opposition. In the same year the Axis alliance between Germany and Italy was signed with Mussolini. Germany was re-arming fast and treated both Britain and France with contempt. For a young man just starting to work in continental Europe it was rather depressing.

Britain and France were slow in responding to Germany's growing power. However Britain had started a substantial naval building programme, among other initiatives. We had also won the Schneider Cup with a remarkable high speed seaplane, from which one of Britain's finest fighting planes, the Hurricane, was developed.

By the time I went overseas, many of my contemporaries in the U.K. had joined various voluntary military organisations, such as the Territorial Army, the Auxiliary Air Force, etc. Always interested in ships and the Royal Navy my own ambition to join HMS President, a Royal Naval Volunteer Reserve training vessel on the Thames, was thwarted by my taking up my new appointment.

Naturally none of us relished the idea of an eventual conflict. It was always hoped the politicians would prevail upon Hitler to moderate his ambitions. Nevertheless there was a considerable degree of nervousness that one might become involved in a war sooner or later. At the age of twenty, one did not take this too seriously as the main aim was to find a job and get on with one's career.

My travels took me to many European countries including, Austria, Belgium, Czechoslovakia, France, Germany, Holland, Italy, and Poland. I was therefore privileged to come into contact and work with people of many different nationalities, and creeds, as well as, to some extent, to understand their fears and anxieties due to the growing tensions in Europe on account of the Nazi menace.

I made my first trip to the Continent in January 1938 to Vienna in Austria where I stayed until the beginning of March before coming to Paris.

When I travelled to Vienna, Gerald Tope was with me to teach the ropes of auditing Gestetner subsidiaries. Gerald had previously been a member of the continental audit staff some years before. He was very kind and helpful and we became firm friends for the rest our time with the Company. Shortly after we had audited the Austrian accounts and produced the balance sheet and schedules in the form required by Head Office in London, Gerald left me with various audit matters to deal with. He returned to London to his job as Assistant Commercial Secretary.

Vienna was among my favourite cities. A very musical city, invariably there would be musicians playing in many of the cafés and restaurants. I enjoyed the opera and other musical shows. In fact I saw the *Gipsy Baron* many times as I was fascinated by a rather attractive lead singer, Margit Bokor, and imagined I was in love with her. Although I never met her — nor do I imagine that even if we had met — my inherent shyness would not have got me anywhere.

I enjoyed going up into the Vienna woods to have my Sunday lunch at one of the many restaurants in the area overlooking the Danube. Sometimes in Vienna I would dine at the famous Drei Hussaren restaurant, which was one of the Duke of Windsor's favourite haunts, although I never met him there.

There is no doubt I saw the better side of Vienna but, out of the bright lights, there was much poverty and distress. Before the Germans took over there had been riots. The Austrian Chancellor, Dolfuss, tried his best but, with Hitler breathing down his neck, he had no chance.

From those Viennese days I suffered the privations afflicting the young Briton abroad, such as getting used to local beers, and strange cigarettes and tobacco. Whilst I became quite addicted to the local beers in the countries I visited, I never appreciated locally made British tobacco brands. The locally manufactured Players cigarettes hardly tasted like the Nottingham product. I got into the habit of collecting book matches and beer mats. I still have an important collection of pre-war book matches but my beer

Beer mats collected during 1938-39, some dated, whilst working as auditor for Gestetner on the Continent

mats have now largely disappeared. I sometimes look at those remaining with nostalgia as I used to date them with the name of the town. Countries tended to have distinctive characteristics such as odours. Vienna had a distinctly sauerkraut odour.

When in Vienna I used to lunch, together with the Company Secretary, at the brasserie of the famous Sacher Hotel. This gentleman was perhaps the only non-Jewish employee in the Vienna office. When the Germans entered Austria, a week after I had left to go to Paris, he declared himself a loyal Nazi and took over the business, as the manager, Herr Gruber, had fled the country. I do not know what happened to the rest of the staff. The Nazi Secretary General was promptly sacked when London was able to regain control of the business after the war.

I was naturally shocked when Hitler invaded Austria just after I had left. Although I knew the political situation between Germany and Austria was pretty bad, I had no idea that an invasion was about to happen. The Anschluss, as the invasion was known, was a terrible thing for the large Jewish population of that country. Although many escaped, most suffered at the hands of the Nazis. This was my first taste of the horror that was unfolding in Europe. I was profoundly moved by the fate of those with whom I had been working only a few days beforehand.

From Vienna I travelled to France for my first visit and met my fellow auditors for the first time. We stayed in a small but comfortable hotel, the Hotel de Bourgogne et Montana, on the little square at the angle of the Rue de Bourgogne behind the Chambre des Deputés, the French equivalent of the House of Commons. Since the war it is now called the Assemblée Nationale.

The hotel had quite a nice restaurant where we soon became well known, particularly for our evening meals. Our offices were in the Rue du Louvre, very near Les Halles, the Central Wholesale Market supplying the entire city. It contained the meat, fish, vegetable and flower markets. An extremely lively and busy part of Paris, particularly in the early and late mornings, it caused traffic jams, much of it horse-drawn. There were some excellent restaurants, and bistrots, surrounding the markets and which were only a short walk from the office. One of the bistrots, Le Soleil d'Or, became our favourite place for lunch. In those days it was customary for the lunch break to last for two hours which gave one plenty of time to enjoy one's meal. The manageress was Madame Madeleine and the food superb. Madeleine was a well known personality on the Paris scene and many of her customers were also well known.

To get to the office we either walked from our hotel across the Seine or took a traditional Paris bus, standing on its typical outside platform.

Gestetner rented their offices in the rue du Louvre. They consisting of a basement where the main stores of paper, stencils and inks were available for delivery to Parisian customers, or for shipments to the several branches — notably Lyons, Marseille, Lille, Rouen, Toulouse, Bordeaux, and Clermont-Ferrand. The ground floor was also used for stores at the rear, with a copying office and showroom to the front. The copying office undertook stencil printing work for casual customers. On the first floor were the executive offices, the Paris sales branch and the accounting section. On the fifth floor there was a small factory which assembled stencils and tubed ink. As far as I can remember the staff of the French company was in the region of 350 at this stage.

I spent more time in Paris than any other city on the continent as France was the company's most important subsidiary in Europe. However, contrary to today's modern France, where the trains run on time, and the health and other services are excellent, my impressions of pre-war France were that, compared with England, and even more so with Germany, there was much evidence of things being rather backward and run down. The armed services did not appear impressive. No doubt the continuous instability of successive French governments was responsible for this but it did not detract from the charm of the country and its culture.

We had to work hard as we were always up against a tight timetable at balance sheet times, for the half yearly results at the end of March, and September for the full year's accounts. We were responsible for establishing the landed cost prices of each saleable item, to price and calculate the inventories, and translate the local French accounts into the form required by Head Office, and to prepare all the relevant schedules which we received from London. These schedules were very detailed, breaking down expenses in detail under several headings per branch of the subsidiary and similarly for the gross profit schedules by branch. In those days there were no calculating machines available so everything had to be calculated by hand, which entailed checking each other's work. It was often necessary to work most of the night to finish on time. Once the balance sheet was out of the way we had to analyse the expenses and gross profits for each branch, reporting on any anomalies, These had to be explained in the reports we typed for London. As soon as our reports were ready we would discuss them with the local manager before sending them, or if required, taking them ourselves to London. Once the management in London had digested them, Gene Strehler, our manager and Mr A. S. Bass (ASB), the Director responsible for the Group's commercial activity, would come over to discuss the results with the local manager and fix his remuneration and bonus.

Gene Strehler was an excellent and patient tutor who was much respected by us all. As soon as ASB had discussed our reports he would say to Gene 'thank the boys and take them out to dinner.' We then enjoyed a very pleasant meal in one of Gene's favourite restaurants.

Thus I found myself plunged into having to understand other languages as well as calculate accurately and quickly. Arithmetic being my weak subject at school, it was not long before I could spot errors and develop a good sense for figures, which was essential for my later career. With some difficulty I could make myself understood in French and did pick up a little German.

In between balance sheet periods we carried out other detailed audits depending on instructions from London.

The manager of the French Company was Charles Ullman, son-in-law of the founder of the Gestetner Ltd, David Gestetner. The chief sales manager was an Englishman, Gordon Plant, and the company secretary a Swiss, M. Rossinelli, or 'Rossi', a very colourful character who kept a bottle of whisky handy in one of his filing cabinets, which he frequently opened.

John Hawtry was senior to both John Cobban and myself. He was a strange aloof person who had a defective eye. He was very conscious of this defect and took umbrage if any stranger stared at him. On more than one occasion he sought to pick a fight with another diner who stared at him in a restaurant; this generally ended with John and I having to apologise for our friend. John Hawtry was passionate about the Royal Navy and made sure that we all knew that. Eventually he left us for promotion to become the Secretary of the Gestetner business based on Singapore. Sadly, during the war when Singapore was captured by the Japanese, he did not survive. However we do know that he joined the local Royal Naval services and are quite certain he acquitted himself with the greatest gallantry. He was that type of person.

On one occasion when we were all together in Paris, one of us, either John Hawtry or John Cobban, became quite ill with the 'flu so we asked the hotel to call a doctor. The doctor told us to apply 'ventouses' (glass cups similar to a yoghourt glass) to his back to draw out the fluid from his lungs. This was something strange for us so we bought a set of ventouse and applied them all over his naked back by heating each glass with lighted cotton wool imbibed with surgical spirit. These caused his skin to swell up inside each cup so that the pores gave out the fluid. The remedy was quite effective and he made a rapid recovery.

The distinctive smells of Paris were French cigarettes and the Metro underground, all mixed with a trace of garlic.

I was instructed to go to Prague with John Cobban in May/June 1938. At that time there was much unrest in the Sudeten, an area of Czechoslovakia largely populated by people of German origin, who, under their leader Heinrich Henlien, were agitating to join up with Germany. This was part of Hitler's plan to create the greater Reich.

I forget the Czech country manager's name but he, like all our managers in Europe, was Jewish, often friends or members of the Gestetner family. The secretary of the company was a Mr Tesar who was very helpful to us, as was the sales manager, Herman Smetana. The latter managed to survive the war and became an important executive in the Firm and for a time my boss in London.

The Czechs are a very musical people. The Czech composer Smetana so wonderfully reflected the beauty and spirit of his country. The office staff were very musical too and would often leave the office with their various instruments to play at a concert or at home with friends.

Prague is a very beautiful city. As we planned to be there for a month or so we hired a flat instead of staying in an hotel. On one occasion we invited some girls from the office to dinner. It was a hilarious occasion trying to teach us Czech. To prepare for our meal we washed the salad in the bath but more than that I cannot remember what we ate.

For our daily lunch we would go to a restaurant which specialised in delicious hot Prague ham and sauerkraut with a glass of Pilsner beer. We would often have several helpings.

During our stay we spent the Whitsun week-end by taking the train from Prague to Marienskilazne (Marienbad) in the heart of the German speaking Sudeten mountain area, some of the most beautiful countryside anywhere. Marienskilazne was and still is a well known international watering spa.

Due to the political situation the place was virtually deserted but this did not stop as from sampling the waters whilst we listened almost alone to some wonderful orchestral concerts. On the way to Marienbad the train stopped at Pilsen where the famous beer is brewed. As the train came into the station there were vendors selling frankfort sausages and glasses of pilsner beer. We naturally took advantage of this.

In Marienbad everyone was very civil until we stopped off for a beer at a fairly deserted café on the outskirts of the town when young men wearing Nazi swastika armbands started arriving greeting each other with a hearty 'Heil Hitler'. Two of them approached us and asked us to leave but we stubbornly said we were going to finish our beer. They then became aggressive and menacing, threatening to throw us out, as they were going to hold a secret Nazi meeting, something which was strictly forbidden in the Czech Republic. Outnumbered, reluctantly we had to go and leave our unfinished beer.

Not long after our visit to Prague, I returned to Paris. In Paris, as elsewhere in Europe, tension was very high and people were beginning to feel the worst was about to happen. I was there at the time of the Munich crisis, in September 1938, when Hitler managed to obtain the agreement of the British and French Prime Ministers, Chamberlain and Daladier, to cede the Sudeten area to Germany. I well remember the sense of relief when Neville Chamberlain descended from his plane on arrival in London from Bonn displaying a sheet of paper of proudly saying 'This piece of paper will bring peace in our time'. Naturally, this agreement was considered by the Czechs to be a betrayal of their country.

I was having a meal at one of the many large café-restaurants on the Champs Elysées when the newspaper vendors came rushing up the street with the news. It was an exciting moment and the feeling of relief from the previous days of international tension was immense. However the relief did not last for long, as Czechoslovakia was eventually occupied by Germany in March 1939. Thus the second country I had recently visited came under Nazi rule.

I visited Germany many times. Contrary to the seemingly more easy-going French way of life, everyone in Germany gave me the impression of going about his or her business with earnest determination. Germans, particularly those in uniform, often appeared somewhat arrogant.

Needless to say, one could not help but admire the way Germany had pulled itself up from those frightful days of depression and rabid inflation. I have a framed cheque drawn on the Berlin office of the American Express Company dated 14th October 1924 in favour of Albert Wilson, my father-in-law, for 9,707,907 Deutsche marks and 13 pfennings to cover his expenses for an assignment at the bank. He did not bother to cash the cheque as it would have cost him more to carry the cash away.

I worked in Berlin many times, sometimes with my colleagues, at others on my own. As Gestetner was considered to be a Jewish company by the German authorities, the German subsidiary could only operate if it could be disguised as a non-Jewish business. This was somehow arranged but controlled from London nevertheless. My boss, Gene Strehler, being a neutral Swiss, was nominated to be a director. The local staff were all German, but not all of them were pro-Nazi. I used to stay at a pension on the Kurfurstendam. The local manager, Herr Joachim, would pick me up in the morning to take me to the office, situated in a rather dingy suburban industrial area. It was only when in his car would this good man express to me his real concern on the way the Nazi regime had taken over the country and its destiny. Other employees also expressed similar sentiments, particularly those who had taken part in the First Great War, but they were extremely discreet about it.

The Kurfurstendam was a busy artery with many shops, a number displaying the "Juden" (Jewish) sign. I was surprised they could still trade although on more than one occasion I witnessed Jewish people being molested and chased in this area. This was just before the "Kristal nacht" — The night of broken glass — on 9-10 November 1938 when Jewish shops, synagogues, and homes were smashed and looted.

Most people in Berlin were wearing a uniform of some sort: army, airforce and navy, SS, and Labour Corps, Hitler Jugend (youth) and so on. There were frequent marches through the streets, the Labour Corps with their spades at the shoulder and the Hitler Youth in their shorts. There were frequent fly pasts of hundreds of aircraft. All these displays of military might tended to give me the jitters, although these demonstrations of power understandably raised the spirits of the German population and their pride in their growing might. Nazi flags and emblems were displayed everywhere.

Hitler frequently made speeches and these were re-broadcast from loudspeakers in the streets. At these times the population would dutifully stand silent to listen. Although I did not understand German, Hitler had a fascinating voice and his delivery even cast a bit of a spell over me as well. Notwithstanding, together with my two colleagues, we used to make a point of ignoring these broadcasts and would elbow our way through the groups gathered round the loudspeakers. This was perhaps rather impolite but no one took much notice of us.

Another time, when I was in Berlin on my own, I booked a ticket for a cinema performance later that evening. As I set off to have a meal at my favourite little restaurant beforehand, Hitler embarked on another important speech. The people in the streets were as usual herded round the loudspeakers, but the broadcast was also being relayed in the restaurant. I had my meal in respectful silence as the great man continued to speak. Finally I decided to creep out for my cinema appointment only to discover that the speech was being relayed in the cinema as well. It went on for a long time, so I fell asleep. I was woken up by being punched in the back for not rising for the national anthem when Hitler had at last finished speaking. Rather foolish, perhaps, but I was displaying a bit of my defiance of the Nazi regime. I explained I was British — *Ich bin ein Englander* —which seemed to satisfy them so I was not arrested. In fact the Germans seemed to tolerate the eccentricities of odd foreigners like me. Nevertheless I was requested to change my seat to view the film.

"Guns and not butter" was the order of the time in this country of Ein Volk, Ein Reich, Ein Fuhrer (one people, one state, one leader). As such the German people had to forego many luxuries and were obliged to put up with ersatz substitutes. For example, one day of the week was set aside as Ein-kopft day when one could only eat a sort of casserole of food made from the scraps of the week.This rule applied as much to restaurants as to private homes and was rigidly adhered to.

The Italienische Taverne in Berlin was always an interesting place to eat or have a beer, as it was the rendezvous for well known international journalists, such as Neville Henderson (not to be confused with the British Ambassador of the same name in Berlin at the time). Henderson's reporting and books were very authoritative on the German scene.

For us working in Berlin was similar to elsewhere; always deadlines to finish a job on time then move on to the next country. The management and personnel at the Berlin Office were always very cooperative and friendly. The offices and sales and technical services were in a hangar at a disused airfield in the suburbs. It was not possible to find a suitable restaurant for lunch in the vicinity so we relied on one or two elderly employees to purchase food for us. These particular gentlemen had fought in the Great War and were by no means happy about Germany's aggressive attitude towards other nations. I believe they were sincere but, like others throughout the country, were afraid to openly express their anxiety.

In retrospect I am sorry I did not take more advantage to explore Berlin as it was a fascinating city with many cultural treasures to visit and enjoy its orchestral and other musical delights. Unfortunately we would waste much of our spare time sitting in cafés, eating, or at the cinema. This was very much our routine in the other countries we visited. Our nomadic life did not make it very easy to get to know anyone very well, so we tended to keep ourselves to ourselves. Berlin was very cold in winter but pleasant in the summer, when one could wander in the Tiergarten Park in the centre of the city, or go out at the week-end to the lakes at Wannesee, a favourite playground for Berliners.

The restaurants were good. The dishes I liked best were chicken soup, roast goose, and Viennese schnitzel. All the time I was adding to my collection of book matches and beer mats. The slight smell of coal fumes was my over-riding recollection of the Berlin air. These fumes were peculiar to Berlin, no doubt due to heating fired by brown coal as opposed to anthracite in England.

Other cities I visited frequently were Brussels and Amsterdam. The Belgian company's offices were in the centre of the city. A Jewish gentleman, Henri Bercovitch, was the manager. Prior to taking over Belgium he had been a salesman and branch manager in the French company. He was a rather forbidding character, not easy to talk to but very effective professionally. He spent a great deal of his time pacing up and down his office, chain smoking his favourite brand of French cigarettes. This was his manner to solve problems. His sales manager was a woman, Madame Clerbois, the wife of one of her salesmen. The Secretary accountant of the business was Madame Baudrier. Both these persons were well respected in the company inside and outside Belgium.

I cannot recollect any particular smell to the Brussels atmosphere. There were some lovely parts of the city, particularly the wonderful Flemish architecture of the Grande Place in the heart of the city. Elsewhere in the Place Bouquerre it was said the fountains stopped whenever a virgin passed by. As the fountains never ceased to flow one could only drawn one conclusion, although I am unaware if a proper study of the question was ever carried out.

My daily expense allowance enabled me to stay in a decent hotel and feed in good restaurants. One evening on leaving a well known restaurant, after I had an excellent dinner, I was a bit embarrassed to come face to face with Henri Bercovitch and Sigmund Gestetner, the Group Chairman, who were also dining there. They were mildly surprised but greeted me well.

At this particular restaurant, but not on this occasion, I discovered that I liked small jerusalem artichokes in vinaigrette, and consumed a handsome quantity. I paid for that by being sick most of the night. Artichokes went off my menu for some years after that.

Our offices in Holland were in Overtoom in Amsterdam, a city we found expensive, so we had to draw on our reserves to satisfy our standard of living. This was partly because we stayed in the rather up-market American Hotel, where we enjoyed the full Dutch breakfast each morning. That is an English breakfast plus Dutch cheese and hams, a welcome change from croissants and coffee.

To get to the office we would walk from the hotel through the Vondel Park to Overtoom. Like all Dutch people Bert Hunink, the manager, spoke excellent English. A tall handsome man, he was a good friend to us. Invariably, we had a snack lunch with him at the American Hotel. I remember he had a bee in his bonnet about beds, saying one should never sleep in a bed over a water course as it would disturb one's sleep. Since then when I have sleeping difficulties, I often wonder if my bed is over a hidden stream, and I think of Bert Hunink.

The Company Secretary and Accountant was Mr Lier, a very active little man who spoke many languages. I got on well with the office staff who often kindly took me sailing, or for a cycle ride into the country. The Dutch cycle everywhere and the cars and trams respect them. Holland is flat so it was obvious that cycling should be easy. Not for me, however, when I was invited by my office friends. There always seemed to be an adverse wind as we cycled along the polders. They were used to it, I was not.

I was attracted to Amsterdam with its many canals and the ships in the port, as well as its quaint buildings. The Rijksmuseum with its masterpieces is a delight.

Dutch food is a bit heavy but generally good. With its Indonesian connections, there were some fine restaurants serving traditional reistaffel food which I particularly liked to eat, providing I had the time to enjoy all the many dishes. Swallowing raw herrings from the street vendors was another enjoyable must. The smell of the canals with traces of fish were Amsterdam's trade mark to me.

Italy, despite the Fascist regime, and its black shirted officials and its busy party members, did not give me the impression of being as menacing as the atmosphere in Germany. The Italians were much more exuberant and spontaneously friendly than their German allies. Whilst they were seemingly united in their allegiance to Mussolini, or Il Duce, they tended to be less aggressively militant. Nevertheless there were frequent parades of Blackshirts and many colourful uniforms. However, one had to remember Italy had recently conquered Ethiopia and had eyes on parts of the south of France. I found Italians delightful individually and they often made fun of their government.

Our offices were in Milan, the commercial centre of the country. The manager was M. Senti, whose son Mario had been a contemporary of mine in London when I first joined the Company. Quite naturally his father delegated Mario to look after us during our stay. Mario had a little Fiat Topolino with which he sped us round town at great speed, showing John Cobban and me the sights and places we might not have seen otherwise.

Mario, a few years older than me, is still very much alive with his wife and son and daughter at the time of writing.

He later took over from his father. I have not seen him since I retired although we exchange cards each Christmas time. One of the sights Mario took us to was a very up-market brothel. The girls were stunningly attractive but we managed to avoid the temptation. I was still a shy virgin in those days and my principles kept me from any thought of such temptation.

(Actually this was not my first visit to a brothel. When in Paris, I accompanied the British Rugby Club of Paris to a game against the Verdun Rugby Club at Verdun. I was a spectator and not a member of the team. We were met on our arrival at Verdun station by the opposing team, who wined and dined us more than well. Afterwards they took us to one of the local brothels. Verdun being in a very highly militarised area in the East, there were many such establishments particularly patronised by the soldiers manning the Maginot line. I thought the inmates of this particular establishment were most uninviting creatures. Some members of our team did stay on after we left; we did not ask any questions the next morning. The Verdun Rugby Club by their hospitality had thus assured themselves of a resounding victory. An interesting experience. I did manage to visit the Great War battlefields, the ossuary Monument at Douamont and the buried trenches as they had been left intact after the war. Very moving but so sad.)

I do not remember any distinctive Milan smell but I suppose there must have been such as pasta laced with garlic. I was still picking up the odd book match.

I was sent to do the audit in Warsaw in June 1939. By then of course the Poles were being harassed by Germany to hand over Danzig as well as other parts of the country. The Polish army was much in evidence and gave the appearance of being very smart, but unfortunately later proved to be no match against the invader. My memory of Warsaw was being struck by the high proportion of Jews in the city. The men, mostly with their traditional long curly side whiskers underneath their flat black hats, wearing their traditional black clothes were very distinctive. Sadly, few could have survived the Nazi regime.

I do not remember the offices in Warsaw nor the name of the manager but I do know he managed to escape to Britain.

International tension was again very high about this time. Britain introduced National Service and I became eligible to register in the first batch of national servicemen. I thought it wise for me to register so did so at the British Embassy in Warsaw but there was no follow up.

Poland was not a very important subsidiary but I carried out the usual balance sheet and audit. I stayed in the best hotel which I understand was owned by the great pianist Paderewski. There is a large square, Pilsudski Place, in the centre of the town, surrounded by cafés and restaurants. Prior to eating my chicken kiev I introduced myself to vodka. A full bottle would be put on your table with a small glass and you paid for the amount you had drunk. I soon found that two glasses was quite enough, otherwise things became a bit unsteady.

Throughout the ages the Polish nation has endured invasions and pressures from all sides. They told me they feared the Russians as much as the Germans. Alas, it was not long after I left Warsaw to return to Paris that Hitler invaded Poland in September. Thus the third country disappeared following my recent visit. Of course later Belgium, Holland and France followed suit.

I returned to Paris and again registered at the British Embassy for national service but nobody seemed interested.

I received a call from Norah Fraser, a school friend of my sister. On their way back to Beckenham from the Argentine, she was staying in Le Touquet with her mother; I was invited to spend the week-end with them. The Frasers were a Scots family of ten children who owned a ranch up-country from Buenos Aires where they normally lived. For the education of their children they had acquired a house opposite ours in

Beckenham. As her mother was often absent in the Argentine Norah almost became a part of my family. She was great fun and much loved by us all. To say that she was my girl friend would be an exaggeration but we were very fond of each other.

Whilst in Le Touquet the international situation became very tense and it seemed war was imminent. I was recalled home by my Company and was able to help Norah and her mother return to England with all their luggage. This was the last time I saw Norah. Together with one of her brothers she had embarked on board a Blue Star liner, the *Andorra Star* to return to the Argentine in 1942. The ship was torpedoed. Some years later my sister learned from a survivor that both Norah and her brother had managed to leave the ship in one of the lifeboats but had become separated from the others. Apparently Norah had been the life and soul among the passengers during the voyage. At the age of 23 we mourned the loss at sea of a very bright and lovable person.

The crisis abated so I returned to Paris to prepare for the June audit. Germany invaded Poland. This was the last straw so Britain declared war on Germany on 3rd September 1939. I was staying at my habitual hotel just behind the Chambre des Deputés. I asked another guest at the hotel, who was a member of the French Parliament, if France was also going to declare war. He told me he thought they would probably follow suit that afternoon; of course, they did, some several hours after Britain.

My Company recalled me to London the day war was declared. I managed to book a seat on the train to Dieppe that evening and spent my last few hours in Paris having a meal in gloom by candlelight. Paris was blacked out. The train took most of the night to get to Dieppe. It was crowded with refugees, including many noisy children. It frequently stopped on the way due to troop train movements. It was very difficult to know where we were in the black-out.

We finally reached Dieppe in the early hours of the morning to be told there were no more boats to England until after the war. A rather distressing prospect but, after one or two air raid alarms, a boat was produced and we sailed away on a beautiful sunny day. On the quay side and all over the town of Dieppe British travellers had abandoned their cars. I often wondered whether the owners ever got them back again. The passengers were told to line the decks to keep on the lookout for mines and submarines.

Back in the U.K. I made my final, but successful, application to register for National Service. I spent a few weeks working at Tottenham and in October 1939 was called up for an interview with the military authorities. They asked which service I would like to join. I asked for the Navy but they said there were no vacancies and that I would have to join the Army. They then asked which arm of the service. I requested the artillery as my father had served with the artillery during the Great War. They said that they would arrange for that but to my surprise I received calling up papers to report to the depot of the Dorsetshire Regiment (The Dorsets) in Dorchester in late October. I was thus destined to became an infantryman.

I thought this was disappointing as my family doctor had previously told me my flat feet and varicose veins would probably render me unfit for the infantry.

Military Career (1939 - 1946)

My years as a member of His Majesty's Armed Forces was a fairly short period of my life, only 6.875%, or six years and five months measured by my age at the time of writing. Of this two years and four months were spent in England learning to be a soldier in an infantry regiment, then learning to be an infantry officer. I then spent the next three years and eleven months in service overseas. Two months on the high seas sailing to Egypt to spend the next eighteen months in North Africa was followed by the remainder of my army life in Italy.

During this time I learned much. To learn to live with and appreciate my fellow comrades. To assume responsibilities at an early age. To experience the excitement of conflict but to know fear and to master it. To wonder why I had so many charmed lives when others were less fortunate. To know the sorrow of loosing friends and comrades and to forever cherish their memory. To witness so many damaged bodies. To maintain my Faith and to thank God for bringing me home well and sane.

This may appear rather dramatic and it was at times. Whilst one is on active service right from the beginning one is keyed up for any eventuality, but I found it quite astonishing how relatively little time both my regiment and myself actually spent in trying to kill our enemy. This was particularly true for the time we were in North Africa but rather less so in Italy.

As a Private soldier, 1939

Dorset, Aldershot, Lincolnshire, Kent
(October 1939 - May 1942)

My military career, or rather my military experience, started, as it did for many Old Tonbridgians, with the School OTC (Officer Training Corps). I prefer to say experience out of respect for those who were professional career soldiers. Although I never excelled at OTC, I did end up knowing what a rifle looked like. This stood me in good stead when I was called up for national service. I travelled by train to Dorchester with a crowd of other young men from the London area who, like me, were wondering what was in store for us. Many of my new companions were tough fellows from the building industry. My time with the Dorsets was a very happy period in which I learned much about my fellow countrymen. We had a delightfully stern but understanding regular army sergeant instructor who achieved wonders in shaping us into becoming soldiers. Plenty of drill and square bashing and oh so many route marches. As the other raw recruits, who joined with me at the same time, had never seen a rifle, I was very soon appointed to be an instructor and promoted lance corporal, unpaid. I was proud of this — my first promotion — and it was not long before I was recommended for officer training.

Dorset is a lovely county and marching around the beautiful Thomas Hardy countryside was a pleasure which my flat feet and varicose veins did not seem to mind. Among the members of my platoon was a youngster who had spent time in a Borstal school for delinquent boys. As I was the only so-called 'posh' person in the platoon he liked to try to annoy me with snide remarks. One day on a route march he overdid it and tried to trip me up. I turned on him and told the 'bastard' to shut up. This so enraged him that he tried to beat me up. Thankfully my builder mates came to my rescue. They were great chaps and genuine friends and I am forever grateful for having been a private soldier with them. In many ways I was sorry to leave my Dorset friends and a regiment with many battle honours. It had been founded by Clive in India with the proud motto 'Primus in Indis'.

From time to time one would be granted leave for a few days. My family naturally were always delighted to have me back at home in Beckenham. They particularly appreciated the generous ration coupons with which the army sent us on leave. Very often I was at home during the air raids on London. When the sirens sounded we would retire for the night to sleep in the cellars which had been reinforced for the purpose. All hell was let loose on these occasions with the sound of the planes, the bombs exploding and the continuous fire of our anti aircraft guns. The house shook and many times it felt as if we had been hit. Sometimes a member of the family would be on air raid duty to extinguish incendiary bombs. It was at times quite frightening until the sirens signalled the all clear. I was very thankful to get back to my regiment and the relative peace of army life. My father and brother Charles did not have a very enviable time when it was their turn to fire watch at Smithfield, in the City of London, during the 'blitz'. Luckily most of the Markets survived without too much damage.

Despite the air raids, the increasing loss of shipping from enemy submarines, the Dunkirk disaster which we somehow styled as a victory, I do not remember we ever thought we would lose the war, although we were naturally very conscious of the dangers which lay ahead. Nevertheless, there were some doubters; there were some who were accused of being 'quislings'. These latter being defeatists in

National Service recruits, Dorset Regiment, 1939

the style of a certain Mr Quisling, a Norwegian gentleman who betrayed his country. There were 'spivs' who worked the black market. The vast majority of our nation gritted their teeth and played the game. Our morale was boosted by some excellent singers, comedians, and entertainers of all sorts from Myra Hess — playing classical piano music at the National Gallery, at times during air raids — to the fun of Flanaghan and Allen, the Itma and the Bebe Daniels and Ben Lyon radio shows, and of course the forces' sweetheart, Vera Lynn. After the fall of France Great Britain fought on alone until the Americans declared war on the Allied side.

I left the Dorsets to join the 167 OCTU (Officer Training Unit) at Aldershot in May 1940. This was shortly after the Germans had launched their offensive in France, beating the Allied armies and pushing the British to evacuate at Dunkirk during the period 26th May to 4th June. Many of the returning troops were sent to Aldershot where tented camps were hurriedly set up. Our training as officer cadets was almost suspended during this time.

We were employed to help in setting up tents and preparing meals for the returning soldiers who came into the camps in a rather disorderly fashion. They were still in their wet uniforms and mostly without weapons. It was a very sad sight to these men, some of whom were inclined to be a bit rebellious and demanding to go home on leave.

A highlight however was when a battalion of Guardsmen came marching in. They were drenched, but with rifles at the shoulder and in perfect order. It was a fine example and a magnificent sight. They were followed by General Alexander, himself a Guardsman. He had commanded the evacuation, and was the last to leave Dunkirk.

The dishevelled soldiers who had been demanding to go home surrounded Alexander to express their discontent. He calmly asked them who had brought them home. The Navy they replied. Well, the Navy is not having any leave, so you are not going to have any leave, replied the General. By his

Lance-Corporals marked for OCTU, Dorchester, 1940

bearing and natural authority General Alexander brought these men back to reality to realize they were soldiers and not a mob. I was so impressed that Alexander immediately became my hero.

Our training as officers was continually interrupted by digging trenches and anti-tank traps in case the Germans would attempt an invasion. I cannot say we were ardent labourers. When the officer in charge was not present, we would detail one of our number to bring a few pints of beer from the pub round the corner to refresh us in this arduous work. In consequence we became rather sleepy and less ardent.

We were once strafed by a stray Luftwaffe plane which did not do any damage. However one of the main attractions was witnessing the dogfights overhead as the Battle of Britain gained momentum.

We all got on well together at OCTU but soon lost contact with each other after being commissioned as officers. I later learned that one of them was awarded the Victoria Cross whilst another, Antony Bridge, was well known for his liberal use of the word 'bloody'. Some years later I was to meet him again when cruising with my wife. After service in India he had taken up Holy Orders. As Dean of Guildford Cathedral he was one of the inboard lecturers. Unsurprisingly he had acquired the nickname as 'the bloody dean'

I was duly commissioned into my county regiment, The Queen's Own Royal West Kent (QORWK) in 1941. I joined the 5th Battalion which was a territorial battalion and had served with distinction in France and had come back from Dunkirk without too many casualties. I was very young and shy and never really felt at home in this 'club' of experienced officers hardened in battle. I did not find it easy to command a platoon of veterans who did not take kindly to this green and inexperienced young officer. We were stationed in Lincolnshire and spent much time on manoeuvres until we were finally sent to defend the coast on the Romney Marshes around Dymchurch in Kent. In those days the army was very short of arms and ammunition. For example, I had a pistol but no ammunition.

Again we had a grandstand view of the dogfights over southern England. We also used the Romney, Hythe and Dymchurch narrow gauge railway to take our laundry into Dymchurch. The train had an armoured wagon with a 'Boys' anti-tank gun. All rather amateurish.

In moving into Kent we became a unit in the South Eastern Army under command of General Bernard Montgomery. He was famous for making us all undergo physical training before breakfast to harden us up.

Not long after I joined the West Kents, Monty called all the officers of his command to a cinema in Maidstone for a briefing. This little man said he was going to give us his appreciation of the current war situation in the first half of his talk and then in the second half his plans to repel a possible German invasion. He said he would not tolerate any interference whilst he was speaking, not even any coughing. He gave us a few minutes to cough and said we could cough again during the interval. There was much blowing of noses and coughing but not a sound afterwards. At the time of this briefing the Germans were at the gates of Moscow, Leningrad and Stalingrad. Monty confidently predicted that if none of these cities fell before the end of the year, 1941, the Allies would win the war. As the situation at the time seemed desperate one could not but admire Monty's confidence. Monty's superior was General Alexander so I felt we were in competent hands.

Despite their efforts the 5th battalion Q.O.R.W.K. did not consider me to be a very good officer. It was not long therefore before I was considered to be an 'excellent' candidate to be transferred to one of the newly formed Reconnaissance Battalions. These were originally formed from the anti-tank companies of regiments in a division. Broadly speaking they comprised a headquarters company and three reconnaissance companies or squadrons of armoured cars (companies were styled squadrons when the Reconnaissance Battalions were renamed as Regiments on becoming a part of the Royal Armoured Corps), Bren gun carriers, and assault troops. Their role was to probe in front of the division to seek and make contact with the enemy, similar to that of the cavalry regiments.

In early 1942 I was posted to join the newly formed 44th Reconnaissance Battalion (later Regiment, or 44 Recce). I held the rank of Second-Lieutenant. Before I left the West Kents I had attended a course at the Small Arms Training School at Hythe which credited me with very high marks for my competence. I was thus considered to be more of an asset rather than otherwise on my arrival at my new regiment.

Thus began my career with the 44 Recce with whom I served throughout the remainder of the war. We were stationed at Otterden in Kent where I joined B Company (later B squadron) which was commanded by Major J. K. Warner, M. C. Although we were constantly short of vehicles and equipment of all types, we managed to put in much training and learning about our new role. As we were all new to the regiment it was not long before we found our identity to form a very happy and proud unit. However there were some odd characters — such as the second-in-command, Major Lord Sysonby, son of Lord Ponsonby. The latter had been King George V's Private Secretary. Major Lord Sysonby did not get on well with our Colonel so he lived apart from Headquarters. We were billeted in Nissen huts in the surrounding woods so it was not long before we were struggling in the mud between huts. Major Sysonby acquired a cement mixer and spent his time building concrete paths which we referred to as Sysostrasses. He was quite a character but it was not long before he was posted elsewhere and, I have no doubt, served very valiantly.

Shortly after arrival I automatically assumed the rank of Lieutenant and not long after that I was attached to headquarters as the regimental officer in charge of small arms training. I was granted the rank of captain and worked part time as Assistant Adjutant. The Adjutant was Captain Norman Edelshain, who became a good friend. Another officer, who was in command of the mortar platoon, was Captain William 'Bill' Hammond, also an ex-West Kent, who became my best friend in the regiment. We both stayed with the regiment until it was disbanded at the end of the war.

Our division, the 44th Home Counties Division, was still a part of Monty's South Eastern Army until it was chosen to be sent overseas. Our corps commander was Major-General Brian Horrocks, one of Monty's trusted generals. The regiment was now stationed near Tonbridge in Kent where we underwent intensive training exercises in country very familiar to me around Tonbridge and Cranbrook.

Naturally the prospect of being posted for overseas caused much excitement as we were at last actually going to war although nobody told us where we were going. A state secret.

I nearly missed embarking with the regiment as, together with Bill Hammond, I was coming back from an evening out at the nearby Hilden Manor Club when I was knocked down by a passing car which skidded on the icy road. I was temporarily concussed. Bill managed to get me back to headquarters where we were billeted. An ambulance was summoned to take me to the military ward at the Kent and Sussex Hospital at Tunbridge Wells. I was there for nearly four weeks, before being sent home on convalescent leave at nearby Cranbrook, where my family were living at my grandfather's farm. The family house at Beckenham had by then been severely damaged during the Blitz on London. My grandparents' house in Beckenham had also been partially destroyed so the family had retired to the country.

On my return to the regiment, I suffered from severe boils and was sent back home on sick leave. I saw the local family doctor who recommended I drink Guinness. Since doing so I have never had any more boils, my good health no doubt sustained by liberal doses of Guinness. Thus fortified I returned to my Regiment just in time to go overseas.

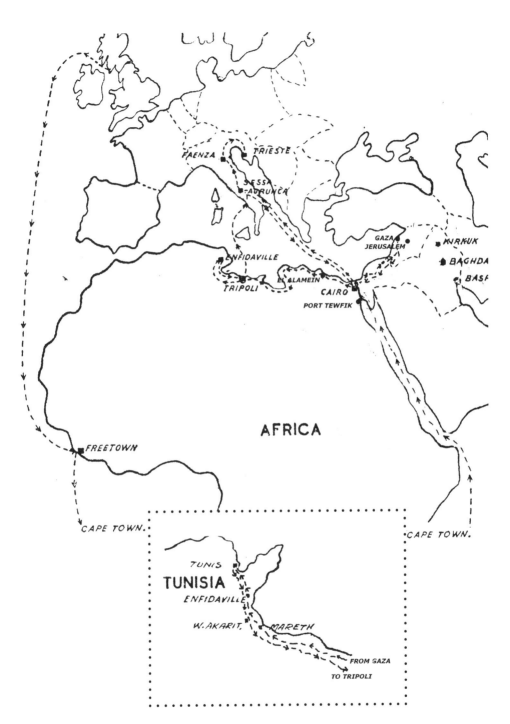

Itinerary of the 44th Reconnaissance Regiment, June 1942-December 1945. UK - North Africa - Italy

En Route for Egypt (May 1942 - July 1942)

After embarkation leave, our vehicles were driven to Liverpool to load onto cargo ships, whilst we took the train to Gourock in Scotland to board an American liner, the *Santa Elena*. The crew were American, supported by elements of the American Navy to man the gun with which the ship was armed. Unlike British ships, all American ships under military control are dry so there was no hope of any alcoholic refreshment during our voyage. However, it was said the only person on board who enjoyed a drink was the American barber, who imbibed the bay rum hair freshener normally reserved for his customers. The *Santa Elena* had been a luxury cruise ship part of an American cruise line fleet, which in peacetime operated on the Pacific coast from San Francisco down to Mexico. It was not built for Atlantic gales. It was a small liner designed to carry only a few hundred passengers. It had been adapted to take nearly two thousand troops so conditions, particularly for the men, were not very comfortable. Extra sleeping accommodation had been built up over the decks to provide for sleeping in hammocks. Meals were American style, everything on the plate topped up with ice cream and with a cup of coffee. There were only two meals a day which were taken standing up. It was necessary to have several successive meal sessions throughout the day to be able to cater for everyone.

The officers fared rather better. We had our own dining room and in my case I shared a cabin with five other officers in bunks two abreast on three levels.

As part of the 44th Home Counties Division, we sailed in a very large convoy at the end of May 1942. I understand it was one of the largest ever, comprising several ocean liners, a battleship (*HMS Rodney*, after her exploits with the *Bismarck* and a refit in the US), cruisers, an aircraft carrier and destroyers. Among the troop carrying liners was *RMS Aquitania*.

It was with some apprehension I watched the changing scene as we sailed down the River Clyde from Gourock to join our convoy in the open sea. Once formed, the convoy sailed due west for several days before turning south in order to give the French coast a very wide berth.

The weather in the North Atlantic was atrocious. I am a good sailor, so I was one of the few who did not suffer from seasickness. I often wonder how I could have survived the stench when inspecting the troops' sleeping quarters. It was also pretty bad in our cramped cabin.

Our constant fear was to be attacked by submarines. During the day the convoy was spread over a vast area —a magnificent sight for me, who loved anything to do with ships. At night, with total black-out, the convoy closed up to avoid scattering and becoming separated, which would have been a gift for a German submarine. Night navigation was tricky and dangerous between ships, being close together with only a small dimmed light shining at the stern of each ship. There were some narrow misses.

Before we left Britain we had been issued with tropical kit including sun helmets so we naturally assumed we were destined for the Far East theatre. As Singapore had fallen in February 1942 there was a potential Japanese threat to India. However shortly after leaving Britain it was announced we would be going to Egypt. On board training and lectures, so far as possible, were then directed to preparing us for this destination.

The trip lasted nearly two months with a stop for refuelling at Freetown in Sierra Leone but we were not permitted to disembark. We remained anchored there for several days in the blistering heat until the convoy set sail for South Africa. Half the convoy, including the *Santa Helena* docked at Capetown, whilst the other half went on to Durban. Capetown is a magnificent setting, overshadowed by Table Mountain. We were able to disembark and spent three glorious days there, royally entertained by the South African people. The voyage to South Africa had been uneventful from air and submarine attack thanks to the wonderful naval protection.

We left Capetown at breakfast time one morning and immediately encountered the enormous waves prevalent on rounding the Cape. Our breakfast shot across the dining room and for the next few days it was not possible to provide any hot meals for the entire ship. For anyone who has not experienced this type of sea these waves which seem like mountains are frightening. Anything movable went crashing all over the ship.

After a while things quietened down, meals were restored as we sailed up the east coast of Africa. From Capetown onwards our naval escort was much reduced, no battleship, no aircraft carrier, just a few destroyers. We were a little nervous though, as Japanese submarines were reported to be operating in the Indian Ocean.

Having left Britain in late May, the 44th Division duly arrived safely at Port Tewfik at the southern entrance to the Suez Canal in late July 1942.

North Africa (July 1942 - September 1943)

After disembarkation at Port Tewfik we travelled by train to an area between Alexandria and Cairo where we started training to become acclimatised for desert warfare. We were there for only two weeks before being ordered to the Alamein line in reserve. On arrival in Egypt we had quickly discarded our tropical helmets as unsuitable headgear. But in the desert we also found our motor cycles and LRCs (light reconnaissance cars) were equally unsuitable and discarded them in favour of jeeps and other scout cars.

At the time of our arrival in Egypt, the German General Erwin Rommel and his Afrika Corps together with the Italian Army, had been halted along the Alamein line. This stretched from the coast to the impenetrable Quatarra Depression some forty miles to the south. The British Forces in the Middle East were commanded by General Claude Auchinleck with General Ritchie in command of the 8th Army. However Churchill had lost faith with Auchinleck and Ritchie. He wanted General Gott to take over the 8th Army; unfortunately he was killed in an air accident. Churchill then decided to make a complete change and relieved Auchinleck of his command, to be replaced by my 'hero', General Alexander, to command the Middle East and General Bernard Montgomery to command the 8th Army. Monty officially took over on 15 August 1942 although he had assumed command a few days before then. He had quickly summed up the situation, saying it would not be long before Rommel would attack again, so he decided to reinforce the Alam Halfa ridge by bringing up the 44th Division.

44 Recce moved off from its camp near Cairo on 14th August and drove into the desert for the first time. I was detailed to drive off in advance to contact the headquarters of the 7th Armoured Division, the original famous 'Desert Rats', so named as their divisional emblem was a jerboa, or desert rat. I was to become the liaison officer attached to this division so drove off along a desert track leaving a cloud of dust in my wake. Before long I was met by a jeep coming from the opposite direction stirring up a similar cloud of dust. When we each lowered our sand glasses to my surprise I met, in the middle of nowhere, my old Gestetner colleague, Pym Ormrod. He directed me to 7th Armoured Division where we parted company, vowing to meet for a drink at a convenient moment later but we never met up again.

On arrival I was attached to the headquarters of 22 Armoured Brigade, a part of 7th Armoured. It was not long before I was given a message to take to Lieutenant-Colonel 'Stinker' Braithwaite commanding 44 Recce. I was provided with an armoured scout car with two drivers to take me there. They lost the way and got bogged down in the sand. Determined to carry out my first active service mission I left my scout car to find my way on foot. Darkness fell, I got lost, and finally came across a truck with a sergeant who could not help me but invited me to spend the night in his truck.

I awoke the next morning to find I was only a few yards from where I was supposed to be. I duly delivered my message which turned to be not very important after all. Imagining I could find my way by the stars I soon learned they moved causing one to go round in a circle. My first desert lesson.

I returned to the 22nd Brigade headquarters where the Brigade Major was quite amused by my failure and lent me a jeep to go and look at the Quatarra Depression. I drove off chasing a gazelle on the way. The depression is an immense area below sea level and quite an amazing moonlike sight, considered impassable for military or any vehicle.

Unfortunately when I returned from this little jaunt my stomach was turning and I felt very sick. The Brigade Major took one look at me and had me evacuated to a hospital in the Delta where I was diagnosed with dysentery. During my absence Rommel, as expected, attacked the Alma Halfa ridge on 31st August, meeting stronger resistance than he had expected. 44 Division infantry suffered casualties in this encounter. 44 Recce was not heavily involved in this battle but nevertheless I missed my regiment's first encounter with the enemy.

After discharge from hospital I was sent to convalesce at Lady MacMichael's convalescent home in Jerusalem. Lady MacMichael was the wife of the British High Commissioner for Palestine. Whilst there I was able to visit most of the Holy places in Jerusalem and its surroundings. We spent much time with fellow convalescents drinking tomato juice at the YMCA across the valley from the King David Hotel as we were forbidden alcohol.

In early October 1942 I finally returned to rejoin 44 Recce which was preparing for the forthcoming Battle of Alamein.

Order of the Day, 23 October 1942

The battle which is now about to begin will be one of the decisive battles of history. The eyes of the whole world will be on us, watching anxiously which way the battle will swing. We give them their answer at once, 'It will swing our way'.

We have first-class equipment; good tanks; good anti-tank guns; plenty of artillery and plenty of ammunition; and backed by the finest air striking force in the world.

All that is necessary is that each one of us, every officer and man, should enter this battle with the determination to see it through – to fight and to kill – and finally, to win.

If we do this, there can only be one result – together we will hit the enemy for 'Six', right out of Africa.

The sooner we win the battle, which will be the turning point of the war, the sooner we shall all get back home to our families. Therefore let every officer and man enter the battle with a stout heart, and the determination to do his duty so long as he has breath in his body.

'AND LET NO MAN SURRENDER SO LONG AS HE IS UNWOUNDED AND CAN FIGHT'.

Let us pray that 'the Lord mighty in battle' will give us victory.

Lieutenant General Bernard Montgomery

Monty's Order of the Day on eve of the battle of Alamein, 23 October 1942

El Alamein (23 October 1942)

The Regiment, now under command of Lieutenant-Colonel Lyon Corbett-Winder, was still attached to 22nd Armoured Brigade. During my absence a special task force had been formed which was named the '44th Reconnaissance Carrier Force'. The role of this force was to clear and lead the way through both the British and enemy minefields as soon as the artillery barrage stopped. It consisted of four separate columns each comprising the regiment's carriers, together with those of other units, preceded by a Valentine tank specially fitted with flails to set off mines. It also included members of the Royal Engineers, whose task was to probe for and clear any mines not set off by the tanks and carriers. Some of the carriers were fitted with a sort of harrow which they dragged along behind them to set off mines and to widen the cleared lanes. Once the these columns had cleared the lanes through the minefields the plan was for the Royal Scots Greys to break through with their tanks.

As the operation would be taking place at night there was intensive training through most October nights. By this time I was second in command of B squadron commanded by Major Pat Nesbitt. As such I was in reserve for the battle but took part in the rehearsals to be ready to replace any officer unable to do so through sickness or injury. The role of these officers was to give directions to the Valentine tank commander on a compass bearing whilst sitting behind the tank's turret. Not a very enviable task.

Monty's plan for the forthcoming battle was to make the enemy believe the main thrust would come from the

Capt Edelshain, Lt. Col. Corbett-Winder, Major Whithington

South. Elaborate arrangements were made to deceive the enemy. Hundreds of dummy tanks and other vehicles were assembled; dummy tracks, pipe lines and ammunition were laid out. These dispositions were carried out in secret, but as the Desert Air Force had overwhelming mastery of the skies it largely kept enemy reconnaissance planes away.

Thanks to reinforcements and a liberal supply of recently arrived American Stuart and Sherman tanks, the 8th Army was in a strong position whilst the Axis German/Italian forces were somewhat weaker and suffering from a shortage of petrol supplies. The Air Force and Navy had sunk many of Rommel's supply ships. Nevertheless it was still going to be a tough job to defeat them.

On the eve of the battle, which took place on 23rd October, Monty issued an inspiring Order of the Day (on page 86) which was distributed to all troops.

There was complete silence in this calm moonlit evening as we waited for the barrage to start. I was about to return to my reserve position and on my way passed the Royal Scots Greys with their tanks lined up to go forward when a solitary piper in full Highland dress played his bagpipes whilst marching up and down the lines. A stirring moment I shall never forget.

At precisely 21h40, 882 field and medium artillery guns opened up a furious barrage all along the 40 mile front from Alamein to the Quatarra Depression. It went on for twenty minutes, then the guns concentrated on specific targets. During this time the four columns of our special force moved forward. They met much stronger resistance, and many more mines, than anticipated. None of the columns managed to penetrate the mine fields except Pat Nesbitt's column which got half-way through. Casualties were heavy but Pat managed to stay on under constant and heavy fire throughout the following day. He was awarded a very well deserved D.S.O. I went up to see him during the day, he was his usual calm self, in total control of the situation. Casualties in officers and men were very high.

Rommel had been ill on sick leave at home in Germany when the battle started but returned hurriedly to take command again. To a large extent the effort in the South did succeed in causing the axis forces to hesitate before realising the main thrust was in the North. Then the Germans, largely due to lack of transport, left the Italians to their fate in the south. The battle of Alamein lasted for twenty days before Rommel withdrew to set up a new defensive position further back.

Our engagement was called off after the breakthrough in the North when we regrouped again as 44 Recce. We pursued the Italians for about 70 miles, capturing them by the hundreds. It was a pitiful sight, as they were without food and particularly without water. In desperation they had drunk all the water from their vehicle radiators.

44 Recce was then withdrawn into reserve to a camp at Mena House just nearby the Great Pyramids. In January 1943 we moved to Cairo, stationed in the Citadel, as troops to protect the General Headquarters (GHQ). This was quite a pleasant job, but necessary as King Farouk was very much pro-German.

Apart from our military duties we were able to enjoy becoming members of the exclusive Gezira country club on an island on the Nile. I also took the opportunity to listen to some excellent concerts by the Cairo Symphony Orchestra. We enjoyed the famous Shepheard's Hotel, and some excellent restaurants. Alas, it did not last long. In February we came under orders to join the 56th London Division with PAI-Force (Persia and Iraq) since there was always the possibility that the Germans might invade those countries for their oil, should the Soviets be defeated in the battle for Stalingrad. That city held until the Germans were finally defeated in February 1943.

Although we came under command of 56th Division at this time we never joined them in Iraq. Instead we were posted to the Gaza area of Palestine for training. On March 24th 1943 the division was ordered westwards to move overland to

Symphony Orchestra Programme, Cairo, 1943.

Sylis
KAH.

B

S P E C I A L   O R D E R   O F   T H E   D A Y

HEADQUARTERS
18TH ARMY GROUP
13th May, 1943

SOLDIERS OF THE 18TH ARMY GROUP

Today you stand as the conquerors and heroes of the North African shores. The world acknowledges your victory; history will acclaim your deeds. British, French and American arms have swept from these lands the last of the German and Italian invaders.

As your Commander in the Field, I add my admiration and gratitude to those of the United Nations for this great victory, which will go down to history as one of the decisive battles of all time.

You have captured a complete group of Armies and their modern equipment :-

> 150,000 prisoners,
> Over 1,000 anti-tank and field guns,
> 250 German tanks,
> Many serviceable aircraft,

and a vast quantity of stores, rations, and equipment of all descriptions, including a very large number of serviceable motor vehicles.

Our Air Forces, which have given throughout this struggle such magnificent support to our Armies, have shot down in combat since 21st April no less than 235 enemy aircraft.

H.R. Alexander

General,
Commander, 18th Army Group.

Order of the Day, 13th May, 1943

Personal Message from the Army Commander

TO BE READ OUT TO ALL TROOPS.

1. Now that the campaign in Africa is finished I want to tell you all, my soldiers, how intensely proud I am of what you have done.

2. Before we began the Battle of Egypt last October I said that together, you and I, we would hit Rommel and his Army "for six" right out of North Africa.

And it has now been done. All those well known enemy Divisions that we have fought, and driven before us over hundreds of miles of African soil from Alamein to Tunis, have now surrendered.

There was no Dunkirk on the beaches of Tunisia; the Royal Navy and the R.A.F. saw to it that the enemy should not get away, and so they were all forced to surrender.

The campaign has ended in a major disaster for the enemy.

3. Your contribution to the complete and final removal of the enemy from Africa has been beyond all praise.

As our Prime Minister said at Tripoli in February last, it will be a great honour to be able to say in years to come:—

"I MARCHED AND FOUGHT WITH THE EIGHTH ARMY."

4. And what of the future? Many of us are probably thinking of our families in the home country, and wondering when we shall be able to see them.

But I would say to you that we can have to-day only one thought, and that is to see this thing through to the end; and then we will be able to return to our families, honourable men.

5. Therefore let us think of the future in this way.

And what ever it may bring to us, I wish each one of you the very best of luck, and good hunting in the battles that are yet to come and which we will fight together.

6. TOGETHER, YOU AND I, WE WILL SEE THIS THING THROUGH TO THE END.

B. L. Montgomery,

TUNISIA, 14th May, 1943.   General, Eighth Army.

General Montgomery's Order of the Day, 14th May 1943

93

join the 8th Army, which had broken through the Mareth Line to push the enemy into Tunisia. 44 Recce left Palestine on the 28th March to meet up with 56 Division. We made the long journey by road through Sinai, Egypt, and Libya to arrive at Enfidaville in Tunisia about 24th April.

As we entered the town we were subjected to heavy shelling, something we did not greatly appreciate after the rather soft time we had been having since Alamein. Until the German surrender, on 13th May, fighting was very intense,particularly in the hills near Tunis, and 44 Recce was very actively engaged. By then I had rejoined B squadron, which was still commanded by Pat Nesbitt until he was sent to Staff College. He was replaced by Major Alec Hambro. It was not long before Alec was severely wounded, so I had to take over in the middle of the battle when we were continually under fire. As soon as possible after the battle I went to see Alec in hospital. He seemed quite cheerful but, sadly, died shortly after. Another fellow officer, slightly senior to me, was appointed to succeed Alec to command the squadron but he declined so I was then given command of the squadron and promoted to Major.

To celebrate the Allied victory a Victory Parade was held in Tunis taken by General Alexander, accompanied by General Montgomery and others from the Anglo-American Army which had landed in Algeria under 'Operation Torch' to attack the enemy's west flank. 44 Recce then returned to Tripoli to prepare for the Italian Campaign.

Thanksgiving in North Africa, 1943

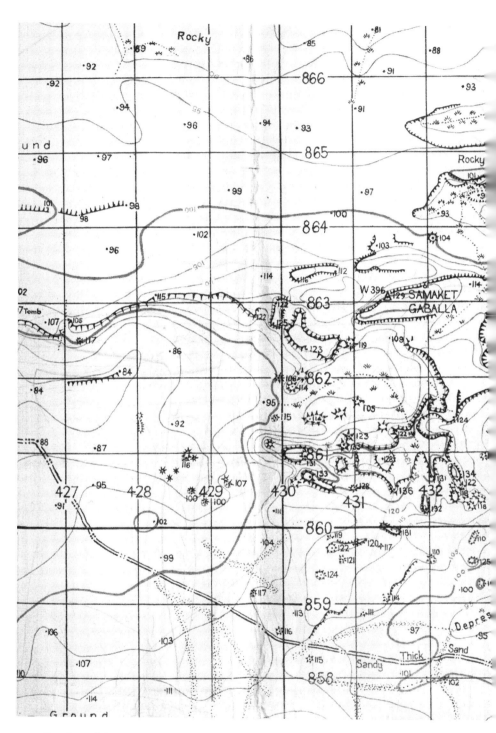

Section of 1 to 50,000 Map, drawn by South African Survey Coy in 1941, and revised by 19th Field Survey Coy in June 1942.

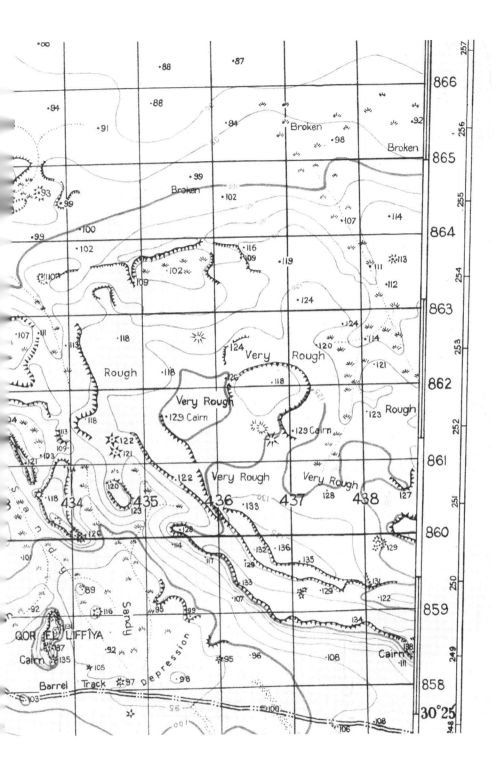

Life in the Western Desert and Egypt

The advantage of war in the Western Desert was that apart from the each side trying to overcome the other, the sand and the rocks suffered, as compared with, later in Italy, towns and villages and their occupants.

The desert had its attractions. Away from the noise of battle a deep and mysterious, almost spiritual, silence prevailed over this vast, never-ending, area of sand and rocky ground. Nevertheless there was life, the occasional struggling vegetation, the sudden display of wild flowers after rain in the spring, the sight of a fleeting gazelle, the charming lazy chameleon until it shot out its long tongue with lightning speed to trap its prey, the strange dung beetle rolling balls of dung to its nest in the sand.

One had to be aware of scorpions, green, yellow and black. A sting from the black scorpion is the most dangerous. I found one which had crept into my bedroll for warmth during the night. They do not sting unless provoked, or after prey. Carefully, I did not provoke mine.

The biggest curse of all were the flies. They got everywhere. It was difficult to keep them off one's food. They settled on the slightest scratch, to produce desert sores which could become sufficiently serious to merit evacuation to hospital. At certain times of the year a flock of geese or some other birds would fly over to their distant destination. Most of the time the climate was pleasantly warm but cold at nights. It could also be quite cold in winter. Sandstorms were another hazard. They were mostly dust storms which would suddenly blow up, sometimes lasting for days. It was like being in a fog. The sand and dust penetrated your clothes, food and everything else.

On the whole I liked the desert but in the beginning I missed my family and used to look up at the moon, believing that if my parents were also looking at the moon I felt there was a comforting feeling of communication between us.

Whilst we were never without water, it was scarce, so there was little available either for our daily ablutions or for the washing of clothes. From time to time, laundry would be sent to the Delta. There were also field units which sterilized our clothing. Mobile shower units were very welcome.

We always carried cans of water, using captured German jerricans if possibie, but we would normally only consume this water in an emergency. One did not drink during the day, except for the inevitable brew-up of tea, but drank as much water as possible around breakfast time because drinking during the heat of day would soon be lost in sweat.

It was a gentleman's war in that both sides accepted the conventions of war. Rommel was a respected commander of the Afrika Corps who likewise respected his opponents. There were no SS battalions in the desert to disregard the Geneva Convention. We unashamedly tuned our wireless sets to listen to Lale Andersen singing the syrupy nostalgic German song 'Lilli Marlene'.

For our comforts we had to put up with Canadian Club whisky and Canadian beer. We smoked locally made Egyptian 'V' for Victory Virginia cigarettes, which nearly caused a mutiny, as the troops hated them and demanded their *Players* or *Woodbines*. The authorities caved in and brought in C to C (Cape to Cairo) cigarettes made in South Africa. We did not care for them either so finally valuable shipping space was found to bring in our *Gold Flake*, *Players* and *Woodbines* from the U.K.

We generally kept in good health but, in addition to desert sores, most at sometime suffered from dysentery, general

Pyramids, 1943
From left to right, on camels, self, Ted Blaber, Pat Nesbitt, Orme Gill,
Dr. Smith

fairly mild, as was my case. Infective hepatitis, or jaundice, to which I succumbed, was quite common too and I had to spend sometime in hospital. British Military Hospitals were always excellent and the nursing sisters a glad sight in this predominately male society.

From time to time there was leave. Either in Cairo, where there was plenty of entertainment, or on to the Suez Canal Zone, which had a very French flavour. On one occasion, together with other fellow officers, we took the luxury night train down to Luxor and spent some very interesting days visiting many of the famous tombs — the Valley of the Kings and the temples at Karnak. We had a wonderful Coptic Christian guide called Ghally Hana. There is something to be said for the old saying 'join the army and see the world'.

The Italian Campaign (10 July 1943 - 2 May 1945)

Wikipedia reminds me that no Campaign in Western Europe cost more than the Italian Campaign in terms of lives lost and wounds suffered by infantry forces.

Approximately 650,000 Allied, including air strength, and, on the other side, 350,000 Axis forces took part. The Allied armies comprised American, British, French, Canadian, Indian, Moroccan, Algerian, New Zealand, South African, Nepalese, and Polish units.

It is estimated that between July 1943 and May 1945, some 60,000 Allied and 50,000 German soldiers died in the Campaign, with a further 320,000 Allied casualties and 336,000 German casualties.

Prior to victory in North Africa there had been much discussion between Roosevelt and Churchill on the best strategy to defeat the Axis. Churchill was in favour of attacking the under-belly of Europe through Italy pending the eventual invasion of Northern Europe, whilst Roosevelt wanted all the Allied effort to concentrate on the invasion of Northern Europe planned for 1943, which would weaken the German pressure on the Soviet front. However this could only be achieved by winning the Battle of the Atlantic first.

Eventually the U.S. and British political leadership took the decision to put off the invasion of France until early 1944 and instead to commit the large trained Allied forces in the Mediterranean to a lower priority Italian campaign. This hopefully might lead to eliminating Italy from the war as well as enable the Allied Navies, principally the British

Navy, and the Allied Air Forces to complete their domination of the Mediterranean sea, thereby massively improving communications with Egypt, the Middle East, the Far East and India. It would also cause the Germans and Italians to transfer troops from the Eastern front to defend Italy and southern France, thus aiding the Soviet Union.

The plan was first to invade Sicily to be followed by the invasion of Italy.

Operation Husky to capture Sicily took place from 10th July to 17th August 1943 with a force of 160,000 Allied forces. Although the Axis forces were beaten, the Germans nevertheless managed to evacuate some 60,000 troops and much of their material across the Messina Straits to the Italian mainland.

We did not take part in the Sicilian campaign. At the time I was still commanding 'B' Squadron, 44 Recce under command of Lieutenant-Colonel Kenneth Hicks. We were stationed near Tripoli in Libya from May to September, to plan and get ready for the forthcoming invasion of Italy. We were still a part of 56 Division, which in turn was a part of 10th Army Corps commanded by Lieutenant-General Brian Horrocks. One of Monty's favourite generals, he was always full of enthusiasm and energy. As was his custom, he came to visit us to give us a pep talk and to explain his future plans. One of his favourite expressions was to ask if we had the 'light of battle' in our eyes. Seemingly we must have given him satisfaction, as he did not berate us for any lack of such light. Keeping those under one's command fully informed of one's plan is an essential part of winning their confidence and in this Horrocks was quite an expert.

Preparations for the invasion included taking 'mepacrine' pills against malaria. Malaria-carrying mosquitoes were very prevalent in certain parts of Italy. It was necessary to take these pills every day. They turned our skin yellow, rather like jaundice. The troops did not like that so it was necessary to adopt a strict discipline when the orderly officer had to ensure they take them at meal times. It was not easy to make sure they had actually swallowed them. Obviously many did not, resulting in a serious number of malaria cases later on, throughout all the forces, after landing in the malaria infested Salerno area.

All our vehicles had to be waterproofed, as they would very likely have to drive through water on disembarking from the landing craft, LCTs (Landing Craft Tanks). These ships, specially designed for the purpose, could carry all my squadron plus a few other troops. They were able to come into shallow water to let down their ramps for the vehicles to drive off.

As the Germans had been defeated in Sicily, it was thought the chosen area for the landings in the Bay of Salerno, south of Naples, would not present great opposition. However, at a briefing just prior to embarkation we were told that the Germans had moved in further new formations. I did not feel so confident that it would be a walk-over after that.

Before sailing General Horrocks was injured in an air raid on Tripoli. Although he recovered later he did not take part in the Italian campaign. He was succeeded by Lieutenant-General Richard (Dick) McCreery.

In between periods of training and preparation I managed to get away to visit the magnificent well-preserved ruins of the old Roman cities — second century B.C. Sabratha and Leptis Magna. These cities on the coast of Tripolitania were originally founded by the Carthaginians in the fifth century B.C.

Itinerary of the 44th Reconnaissance Regiment - Italian Campaign, September 1943 - December 1945

Salerno, 9th Sept 1943

I was now about to take part in the Italian Campaign, in which my Regiment served with distinction, although we were not directly involved in most of the most intensive major battles such as Monte Cassino, the Anzio Landing, and the Battle for Rimini. These were some of the fiercest during all the war. Although the Allies were greatly superior in numbers the Germans had the advantage of a series of well prepared defensive lines across the mountainous terrain, with its many rivers. Much of the time the weather was atrocious, especially in the winter, and often contributed to much delay. These defensive lines which had to be overcome after the Battle of Salerno were, successively, the Volturno Line, the Gustav Line, the Caesar Line, the Albert Line, the Heinrich Line and finally the Gothic Line.

As a motorised reconnaissance regiment, it was not often that we could operate as such, as the Germans systematically blew up all the bridges as they retreated. These had to be repaired or replaced rapidly by Bailey bridges — a British invention of metal sections which could be rapidly assembled by the Royal Engineers. A bridge capable of supporting tanks could be assembled overnight. As a consequence we were often employed in various roles as infantry, special task forces, or holding secondary fronts to enable other forces to mount an attack.

In this context the invasion, code-named 'Avalanche', took place. My squadron embarked at Tripoli harbour and set sail to join the invasion armada of hundreds of ships of all types.

During the crossing we heard that Italy had surrendered. This was very heartening as we imagined we would then be able to sail straight into Naples. It was not quite like that, as we were reminded when a German aircraft fired on us during the night before the landings, luckily without any casualties.

The invasion at Salerno was undertaken by the 5th United States Army under U.S. General Mark Clark with the British 10th Army Corps under his command. The remainder of the 8th Army, under General Montgomery, had landed in the South of Italy to move up the East coast. The 8th Army met little opposition to start with, and quickly occupied the port of Bari on the Adriatic as well as the airfields around Foggia.

All seemed quite quiet as our LCT took up position in the Bay of Salerno at dawn on a magnificent calm sunny day. The massive display of hundreds of warships, different types of landing craft, and hospital ships was most impressive and reassuring. The battle commenced on 9th September. By the time we arrived, the first wave of troops had landed to secure the beachhead but had met with heavier resistance than expected.

Our role was to land with our armoured cars, carriers, and other vehicles as soon as the first wave had moved sufficiently inland. As the first wave was held up, it was not possible so we had to remain on board for a time. Out in the Bay warships were shelling the Germans who were able to oversee the armada and battle area from the mountainous hills overlooking the Salerno plain, over which the invading forces were making very slow progress. Among the warships was the gallant old *HMS Warspite*, a 1914-18 battleship, with its 15-inch guns firing into the hills. As they fired we could clearly see their enormous shells flying overhead as they seemingly made their leisurely way towards their targets.

On D+1 our turn came to move to the beach to disembark. The operation went well, without any casualties, but it was a gruesome sight to see the havoc around about, especially

The grave, in Salerno Cemetery, of my step-cousin, Roy Follit, who died aged 26 in 1943

the effect of German flame throwers. Once ashore, my role with B squadron was to advance with my armoured cars and carriers to take over the so-called tobacco factory (which in fact was a tomato canning factory) near the small town of Battipaglia, in the middle of the Salerno plain, and advance further forward with the Guards Regiment. However this was not possible as the advancing Guards and a Royal Fusiliers regiment, which had previously captured the tobacco factory, were driven out by a German counter attack. They were forced to withdraw to a rear position. As we could not move forward, we were then crammed into a field, together with units of the American army in the bridgehead area.

The whole area was infested with mosquitoes. Thanks, no doubt, to the mepacrine tablets we had been taking, the mosquito-repellent ointment with which we smeared ourselves, and the anti-mosquito bivouac tents with which we had been issued, we had few malaria casualties. However, this was not the case for some units, where the number of cases of malaria was quite high.

I chatted to two of my officers on 13th September; it was night and we were thinking of bedding down. After a while I left them to return to my command car. An enemy plane flew over, showering us with anti-personnel grenades. These flutter to the ground and explode. We suffered two casualties — unfortunately, the two officers with whom I had just been chatting. They received fatal injuries. I was lucky.

This was a great loss; by the time we had evacuated them it was quite late. I then received an order to report to regimental headquarters. The Colonel briefed me on the situation and I was ordered to reorganise my squadron to be ready to take over from the survivors of the 9th Royal Fusiliers, who had fought magnificently but had suffered heavy casualties at the front. Although we would move in with most of our vehicles, it was necessary to prepare for as many men as possible to act in an infantry role.

On my return, together with my officers and squadron Sergeant-Major, we spent the rest of the night reorganising the squadron for this unaccustomed role. At first light I made contact with the Fusiliers to reconnoitre the ground and to make arrangements to take over that evening. Having spent most of the night without any sleep, I was beginning to feel quite tired, so to refresh myself on the way back to my squadron I stopped off at a field of tomatoes. As I was indulging in eating my favourite fruit, up pops a head from the other side of a row of tomato plants to introduce himself as Colonel Twisleton-Wykeham-Fiennes, commander of the Guards regiment. I thought his name was a joke; I found out later that he came from a very distinguished military family. We ate our tomatoes and went on our respective ways.

On my return to the squadron I gathered all my officers and men around me to brief them on the situation and to issue my orders. I had quite an audience — the surrounding Americans were curious to witness a British officer giving his orders. Once this was done I was at last able to snatch a few hours' sleep.

We took over the position as planned on the evening of 14th September without any problem. Our position was quite well camouflaged in a sort of orchard of citrus fruit. The forward positions were dug in behind a farm track with a farm house on the left flank and a wooded area on the right. In front there were tomato and tobacco crops and beyond them we could see the Battipaglia 'tobacco' factory. I made sure everyone knew their field of fire and together with my New Zealand gunnery officer, Captain 'Nick' Straker, we arranged for the forward defensive fire lines to bring in fire from the guns further back in case of attack. The first night was very calm but soon after dark on the second night we could hear enemy tank movements on our front.

At dawn on 16th September we were subjected to heavy enemy shell, mortar, and machine gun fire. The shells and mortar bombs were bursting all around us. Red, green and white streams of tracer bullets were coming at us. Leaves and branches were being torn off the trees as the enemy made attempts to overwhelm us. The situation became serious so I called for intense gun fire on the advancing enemy which Nick Straker calmly directed from his forward observation position. Even the naval ships in the bay were giving us support. Our telephone lines to the forward positions were cut by the enemy gunfire and our troop wireless sets were not working well which made it difficult to control the situation so we had to resort to runners.

My command car was riddled with bullets and collapsed but its wireless was still working, enabling me to keep contact with HQ from a trench beside the vehicle. In the course of running over to contact one of the positions I dropped to the ground as I saw an advancing German trying to take a shot at me. He missed.

Whilst I was on the ground a shell burst behind me. I did not feel anything at the time but a small piece of shrapnel pierced the sole of my left boot and into the sole of my foot. I soon found it painful to walk without the support of a rifle to act as a walking stick.

The battle raged all day. One of my armoured cars was hit, setting it on fire and killing its occupants. To keep in touch with H.Q. my wireless operator, Corporal Pike, did his best to maintain contact. He was a great chap, but always when the action started, it upset his tummy, so he invariably had to clamber out to relieve himself. A brave necessity.

Eventually the enemy infiltrated our forward positions so I ordered my troops to withdraw to a position along a ditch just behind our orchard. Nevertheless, thanks to our resistance and the immense support from the guns, the enemy had suffered severe casualties and withdrew before the end of the day.

The Guards brigade commander, Brigadier Arkwright, came up as we were beginning to sort ourselves out, evacuate the wounded, and recuperate our vehicles. He congratulated us and told me to go for treatment for my wound. I was reluctant to leave my squadron as I did not feel I had been badly wounded, whereupon he gave me an order to go to the Advanced Dressing Station on the beachhead.

I was there for several days whilst they tried to find and dig out the piece of shrapnel in my foot. I found this process more painful than walking with the shrapnel in my foot, providing I was careful to avoid pressure on that part of my foot, so I discharged myself to return to my squadron. As I needed a change of clothing, I told my batman to bring me my knapsack from my armoured car which had taken a battering. (It is customary for knapsacks to be strapped to the outside of a vehicle.) When I came to put on my clean clothes and battledress they were riddled with holes and tears from all the machine gun fire and shrapnel they had received. My clothes resembled those pieces of paper from which entertainers cut out bits to form some sort of pattern. My quartermaster soon provided me with a new outfit.

Within a few days of my being wounded my family received a War Office telegram, and a little later a letter to say that the wound was not serious.

About two months after this action, when we had been withdrawn to prepare to join 56 Division, which had been sent to reinforce the Anzio bridgehead, I was summoned to report to the Colonel, Ken Hicks. Thinking this might concern our marching orders for Anzio I was taken to the Colonel by his batman and surprised to be greeted by him as he stood, stark naked, in a tin tub having a bath. He said, 'I have something for you, Gyles', and pinned the Military Cross brooch on my jacket. I was surprised, as I had no idea I had been recommended for an award. Naturally one is very pleased and proud but humble at the time as one is rewarded thanks to the bravery of many and not just one person.

As I was not able to receive the medal in Italy it was sent to my family home but I received a congratulatory letter from H.M. King George VI.

THE MILITARY CROSS

Captain (Temporary Major) Oliver Giles Longley (149037),
Reconnaissance Corps

—

On 16th September 1943, Major Longley was commanding a
Squadron holding a position South-West of Battipaglia.

During the morning a strong enemy attack, preceded by
mortar and artillery concentrations, was launched on this
position.

The position was held in spite of very heavy enemy
fire, until the enemy had succeeded in penetrating on each
flank and the Squadron was nearly surrounded.

In spite of the difficulties of communication (owing to
wireless sets being knocked out), Major Longley succeeded in
extricating his Squadron and rallying them in a reserve
position some five hundred yards back.

During the action Major Longley, although slightly
wounded, showed outstanding powers of leadership, courage
and determination which were an inspiration to his Squadron.
It was largely due to the fine example set by Major Longley
that the Squadron maintained its fighting efficiency under
particularly difficult circumstances and was successful in
inflicting heavy casualties on the enemy.

Citation for the Military Cross, 17th September, 1943

POST OFFICE TELEGRAM

Charges to pay — s. — d.
RECEIVED

No. 795
OFFICE STAMP

Prefix. Time handed in. Office of Origin and Service Instructions. Words.

PYCC. 2.35. Liverpool Y. OHMS 46

From ___ To ___

redirected from BDS

(Priority CC) Longley Esq. Copthorn
Kingswood Rd, Bromley.—
Regret to inform you of report dated
20th September 1943 received from
Central Mediterranean Area that Major
OG Longley reconnaisence Corp. has

For free repetition of doubtful words telephone "TELEGRAMS ENQUIRY" or call, with this form at office of delivery. Other enquiries should be accompanied by this form and, if possible, the envelope

B or C

POST OFFICE TELEGRAM

Charges to pay — s. — d.
RECEIVED

No. ___
OFFICE STAMP

Prefix. Time handed in. Office of Origin and Service Instructions. Words.

continued

From ___ To ___

been wounded in action stop.
letter follows shortly. stop. —
Under Secretary of state
for War

For free repetition of doubtful words telephone "TELEGRAMS ENQUIRY" or call, with this form at office of delivery. Other enquiries should be accompanied by this form and, if possible, the envelope

B or C

War Office Injury Telegram, 21st September, 1943

Tel. No.: Liverpool Wavertree 4000.

Any further communication on this subject
should be addressed to :—

The Under Secretary of State,
    The War Office,
        Casualty Branch,
            Blue Coat School,
                Church Road, Wavertree,
                    Liverpool 15.

and the following number quoted :

Our Ref./ **OS/2418/L.** (Casualties)

Your Ref./

THE WAR OFFICE,

CASUALTY BRANCH,

BLUE COAT SCHOOL,

CHURCH ROAD,

WAVERTREE,

LIVERPOOL 15.

27th September, 1943.

Sir,

    In confirmation of War Office telegram dated the 24th September, 1943, I regret to have to inform you that a report dated the 20th September, 1943, has been received by telegraph from the Military Authorities in the Central Mediterranean that your son, Major O.G. Longley, Reconnaissance Corps, has been wounded in action.

    No particulars as to the nature of the wound or the name of the hospital to which your son has been admitted have been furnished. If, however, he becomes seriously ill as a result of his wound, further reports will be received by telegraph which will be telegraphed on to you. In the absence of such a communication it can be assumed that your son is making normal progress, in which event you will, no doubt, hear from him in due course about his wound and progress.

    In the meantime communications for your son should continue to be addressed to him at his unit where arrangements exist for their re-direction if necessary.

    Will you kindly notify this office of any change in your address, in case further reports are received.

        I am, Sir,
        Your obedient Servant,

        A.Williams

- Longley, Esq.,
   5, Overbury Avenue,
      Beckenham,
         Kent.

Confirmation of injury by the War Office, 27th September, 1943.

For this same action, on 16th September, I had recommended my gunnery officer, Captain Nick Straker, for an award for his outstanding bravery in directing fire on the enemy whilst he was himself under constant enemy fire. I was delighted that he was also awarded an immediate M.C.

The Eighth made contact with the Fifth Army by the 18th September but already the Germans had started to withdraw from the Salerno area to their defensive line on the Volturno river.

THE WAR OFFICE,

LONDON, S. W. 1.

Any further communication on this subject should be addressed to :—
The Under-Secretary of State,
The War Office
(as opposite)
and the following number quoted.

68/Gen/7772/25(M.S.3)

Your Reference.....................

12 January, 1944.

Sir,

In reply to your letter of the 6th January 1944, I am directed to confirm that The King has been graciously pleased to approve an immediate award of the Military Cross to your son Capt.(T/Maj.) O.G.Longley, Recce.Corps, in recognition of gallant and distinguished services in Italy.   It is anticipated that an announcement of this award will be published in the London Gazette in about a month's time.

In accordance with your request, I have pleasure in enclosing a copy of the statement which was submitted by the General Officer Commanding-in-Chief 15 Army Group, in support of his recommendation for this award.

I am, Sir,
Your obedient Servant,

Lieutenant-General,
MILITARY SECRETARY.

C.W.Longley Esq.,
The Oast Cottage,
Wilsley Pound, Cranbrook, Kent.

Letter to my father, on my being awarded the M.C.

BUCKINGHAM PALACE.

I greatly regret that I am
unable to give you personally the
award which you have so well earned.
I now send it to you with
my congratulations and my best
wishes for your future happiness.

George R.I.

Lieutenant-Colonel O.G. Longley, M.C.,
Reconnaissance Corps,
Royal Armoured Corps.

George VI's congratulatory letter on being awarded the M.C.

After Salerno (October 1943 - July 1944)

When I returned to my Squadron we were for a short while able to operate as a reconnaissance unit, to keep in touch with the enemy as they were retreating to the Volturno Line. Unfortunately, I was not able to take part in the crossing of the Volturno, as I was stricken with diphtheria and evacuated to the American hospital in Naples. The city had only just been captured on 1st October.

The Americans had commandeered the main hospital of Naples. As the hospital had received my medical history from the British they decided to investigate my foot whilst treating me for diphtheria. I was alarmed when they seriously suggested an operation. Luckily I was transferred to a British army hospital to complete my treatment when a nursing sister took one look at my foot and painlessly extracted a small piece of shrapnel which had worked its way to the surface. As I had for some time been walking awkwardly on the side of my foot this has caused me much trouble in later life.

In hospital in Naples I had an excellent view from my bed of Mount Vesuvius erupting. It had been erupting, shooting red hot lava into the air and covering the surrounding area with volcanic dust for some weeks. A very impressive sight at night time. Vesuvius has not erupted again since those days.

For convalescence from diphtheria I was transported by an American ambulance plane to Catania in Sicily. There was a slight hitch on arrival, as the pilot managed to clip his wing on a hangar whilst manoeuvring on the tarmac. It was not serious but a bit disturbing to watch as I lay on my stretcher in the plane. I was taken to a most delightful convalescent home at Taormina from which I was able to study the constantly smoking Mount Etna, yet another volcano.

No doubt if I were to consult the War Diaries of the 44 Recce I could give a day by day account of the Regiment as it advanced to Rome, across the Appenines to the Adriatic coast and thence on to Venice, by which time the Germans had surrendered in Italy, then on to Trieste to protect the Italian frontier from an aggressive Yugoslavia.

This would be rather boring so I will try to give an impression of what 44 Recce did and the circumstances in which we fought the Italian Campaign after Salerno.

On account of the mountainous terrain all the way up to the River Po basin in the North of the country the Germans had the advantage of being able to establish well prepared defensive lines. Unlike the war in North Africa, which was primarily a war of movement with armoured vehicles, in Italy it was much more an infantry and artillery war, at times not dissimilar to the 1914-18 War.

As Reconnaissance regiments were not well suited to this type of warfare we were on many occasions obliged to leave our vehicles to act in an infantry role. Although we saw plenty of action we were not, except on the fringes, engaged in the heaviest battles, some of which were the bloodiest in the war. We spent much of our time on special operations, holding defensive positions, and patrolling, in addition to the occasional moments when we could deploy in our proper role. Nevertheless we were involved in many fierce clashes with the enemy and played an important role as the Allies slowly advanced up the Italian peninsula. The advance was greatly hampered by the atrocious weather, particularly in the winters of 1943 and 1944. This was an added advantage to the enemy as transport was slowed down by mud, and also by the Germans flooding the lower marshland and coastal plains. There were many rivers flowing down from the mountains which rose dramatically with the torrential rain. Naturally, as they retreated the enemy blew up all the bridges.

Although, most of the time, the Allies had an overwhelming superiority in men and equipment compared with the Germans, the latter had the immense advantage in a defensive war under these conditions.

Eventually the Germans abandoned the Volturno Line to take up new well-prepared positions along the Gustav Line which stretched from near Gaeta north of Naples to near Ortona on the Adriatic coast. In advancing to this new line we did manage to keep contact with the retreating enemy in small-scale actions liberating small towns and villages on the way. On one of these actions A squadron even managed to surprise a German sapper party preparing to blow up a bridge. The sappers were captured and the bridge taken intact.

As we progressed the local population greeted us with great joy and were sometimes helpful in pointing out enemy positions. On one occasion as we had settled into a new position based on a farmhouse, I wandered down a track to see some of my men when I stepped on an S-mine. These are anti-personnel mines buried in the ground with three tiny prongs sticking out. When I heard a click, like a twig snapping, I realised I would be dead in the next second or two. The mine jumped out of the ground, glanced on my chest but miraculously failed to explode. It took me a few seconds to realise I was still alive. My luck made me quite famous for a time and even the Colonel showed some emotion on my escape from one of these deadly devices. Even today when I step on a twig and hear that crack my mind goes back to that day.

56 Division had the task of taking Monte Camino, a hill dominating the low ground before the Garigliano river, which the Germans were holding as an outpost to their main Gustav Line defences behind the river Garigliano. The plan was to capture this hill as part of the plan to break through the Gustav Line before winter set in. For this operation elements of 44 Recce were given a new role

to act as porters to supply the attacking infantry brigades, whilst others, including my B squadron, held a part of the line and patrolling. One of the Regiment's officers, Captain - later Major - Peter Osmond, a South African officer who had been seconded to us, volunteered to undertake a two-day personal patrol behind the German positions. He returned with valuable information on 30th November. A few days later he carried out a similar patrol with equal success single-handedly killing or capturing twelve Germans. Peter was heartily congratulated by the Divisional Commander, Major-General G.W.R.Templer. He was naturally famed as an inspiration to everyone but he remained a modest and resourceful regimental officer as second in command of A squadron. When asked to explain his success his answer was that from an early age he was accustomed to tracking game in Africa when it was necessary to approach one's quarry with stealth. Tracking Germans was to him much easier. For his patrols he would take a rifle and a few rounds, a pocket full of cigarettes and a pocket full of chocolate. He was awarded the M.C.

Following the Monte Camino event the Regiment was withdrawn to spend Christmas 1943 in reserve in the area of San Donata and Falciano.

On the 8th January 1944 the regiment returned to action as part of 'Hicksforce', named after our Colonel. In addition to 44 Recce this force was reinforced by elements of other units to take over the coastal sector south of the Garigliano to carry out extensive patrolling. This lasted for about a week, during which a few prisoners were captured. We also had to contend with snipers. One morning, whilst I was shaving in the open behind a building which I thought was quite safe, a bullet smashed into the wall narrowly missing my head. I quickly went inside to finish my shave and to organise a sniper hunt, which failed to find anyone. Hicksforce was part of the plan for the main attack to cross the Garigliano in which 56 Division played an important

Major Peter Osmond, M.C., and Lt.'Nobby' Clark

role. This attack took place on 17th January 1944. 44 Recce crossed on foot the following day with A and C squadrons whilst B squadron was in reserve. C squadron occupied the San Salvatito feature on the left flank of the hills north of the Garigliano. They had done well but were being shot at by snipers. With B squadron I was called in to make a sweep up the hill behind a moving artillery barrage as we clambered up. It was quite frightening as the shells started falling short. We finally made contact with Major Ted Blaber and his C squadron as he exclaimed 'about time too'.

Ignoring his taunt we passed through his lines when I gave the order to fix bayonets as we swept through to the top of the hill bayoneting bushes, and every other possible hiding place. As is often the case on such occasions we did not kill anyone as they fled as we advanced. Sadly we lost a very good young officer who was killed by our own artillery shells which were dropping short. We then returned back across the Garigliano into reserve. On account of heavy rain the river had swollen so much that the Engineers manning the pontoon bridge we had to cross feared it might be swept away any minute. Thankfully it held for us but was washed away shortly after.

B Squadron was again back in action north of the Garigliano. When supported by tanks it attacked and took a German position without loss.

Later in January we were relieved to the rear to re-organise with new vehicles, but plans were changed when we were detailed to return on foot to relieve one of the infantry regiments in the area of San Lorenzo. During February the Regiment carried out numerous patrols, captured a number of prisoners but sustained many casualties. The regiment was commended by the divisional commander for its work in its unaccustomed role acting as infantry.

The Germans fell back to their main defences on the Gustav Line, based on Monte Cassino, which dominated the route to Rome. There were four battles before the Monte Cassino position was taken. The first was in January 1944, the second in February, the third in March, and the final battle May. These battles were some of the most costly during the war and fought successively by American, British, New Zealand, Canadian, French and Polish forces. A diversionary seaborne landing was made by American and British forces in January 1944 near Anzio, south of Rome. In anticipation the Germans had reinforced this area; another extremely costly battle raged until a final breakout in May was possible.

In February 1944, 56th Division, without 44 Recce, was withdrawn and sent to reinforce the Anzio bridgehead in early February 1944. The situation at Anzio had become very difficult. The Division fought there until the end of March when it was withdrawn to return to Egypt for rest and refit.

In the meantime 44 Recce remained in Italy and took up a defensive position west of Monte Cassino in early March 1944 from where we had an excellent view of the bombing of the mountain. It was a fantastic sight as wave after wave of bombers released their bombs but one did wonder if bombing the Monastery was right. Our role, again acting as infantry, was to hold a long line extending to the sea where we carried out a number of patrols and were subjected to a fair amount of mortaring and shelling.

One day I was taking a nap outside my headquarters when a lump of metal fell beside me with a resounding thump. It was part of a German plane which had been shot down. The pilot bailed out and landed in a tree nearby. He was in great pain with a dislocated shoulder. We managed to hoist him out of the tree and evacuate him to hospital. He was extremely young. The plus side of this incident was that I recovered his parachute and had a nice pair of silk pyjamas made from it. We were relieved by the Goums, French Moroccan troops, at the end of the month. The night before they took over, their commander, General Juin, met me to reconnoitre the position. He was a very pleasant person who went on to become a French Field Marshall. It was from here

Personal Message from the Army Commander

Great events lie ahead of us. All round Hitler's Germany, the Allies are closing in: on the East, the victorious Russians drive on — in the West, the British and American Armies are massed to invade.

— Now in the South, the Eighth and Fifth Armies are about to strike.

Side by side with our French and American Allies, we will break through the enemy's winter line and start our great advance Northwards. Our plan is worked out in every detail — we attack in great strength, with large numbers of tanks and guns, supported by a powerful American Air Force and our own Desert Air Force.

The peoples of the United Nations will be watching the Eighth Army. Let us live up to our great traditions and give them news of fresh achievements — great news such as they expect from this Army.

We welcome gladly to our ranks those Divisions whose first fight this is with the Eighth Army. We send a special message to our Polish Corps, now battling beside us to regain its beloved country.

I say to you all — Into action, with the light of battle in your eyes. Let every man do his duty throughout the fight and the Day is ours!

Good Luck and God Speed to each one of you!

Oliver Leese.

ITALY,
MAY, 1944.
Lieut.-General.

Lieut-General Oliver Leese's Order of the Day prior to 4th and Final Battle for Monte Cassino - May 1944

Soldiers of the Allied Armies in Italy

Throughout the past winter you have fought hard and valiantly and killed many Germans. Perhaps you are disappointed that we have not been able to advance faster and farther, but I and those who know, realize full well how magnificently you have fought amongst these almost insurmountable obstacles of rocky, trackless mountains, deep in snow, and in valleys blocked by rivers and mud, against a stubborn foe.

The results of these past months may not appear spectacular, but you have drawn into Italy and mauled many of the enemy's best divisions which he badly needed to stem the advance of the Russian Armies in the East. Hitler has admitted that his defeats in the East were largely due to the bitterness of the fighting and his losses in Italy. This, in itself, is a great achievement and you may well be as proud of yourselves as I am of you. You have gained the admiration of the world and the gratitude of our Russian Allies.

Today the bad times are behind us and tomorrow we can see victory ahead. Under the ever increasing blows of the air forces of the United Nations, which are mounting every day in intensity, the German war machine is beginning to crumble. The Allied armed forces are now assembling for the final battles on sea, on land, and in the air to crush the enemy once and for all. From the East and the West, from the North and the South, blows are about to fall which will result in the final destruction of the Nazis and bring freedom once again to Europe, and hasten peace for us all. To us in Italy, has been given the honour to strike the first blow.

We are going to destroy the German Armies in Italy. The fighting will be hard, bitter, and perhaps long, but you are warriors and soldiers of the highest order, who for more than a year have known only victory. You have courage, determination and skill. You will be supported by overwhelming air forces, and in guns and tanks we far outnumber the Germans. No Armies have ever entered battle before with a more just and righteous cause.

So with God's help and blessing, we take the field—confident of victory.

H. R. Alexander

General,
Commander - in - Chief,
Allied Armies in Italy

May, 1944

General Alexander's Order of the Day, May 1944

Order of the Day.
===========

by

BRIGADIER A.F.L. CLIVE, DSO. MC.

Commander 24 Gds Bde Gp

- - - - - - - - - - - - - - - - - - - -

1.   During the past four weeks the Bde Gp has been occupying a quiet part of the Italian front. This has not necessarily meant a lazy time for all concerned, though it has not been unpleasant for the majority.

2.   A great deal of hard and sometimes dangerous work has been carried out by Battalions, accompanied often by other arms, both in alert observation and on patrol, and this is fully appreciated by the higher commanders.

3.   I wish particularly to mention the patrols of No 2 Coy 5 Gren Gds, of RF 1 SG to Monte ARARECA, and of No 4 Coy 3 Coldm Gds beyond ALFADENA. All these are deserving of high praise. Good patrolling can only be successfully accomplished by brave and determined men.

4.   Now that the offensive in Italy is about to begin again, and in spite of the fact that we are, for the time being, only onlookers, we must be prepared at any moment to play our part whether it be passive or active; AND WE MUST NEVER RELAX. Only thus shall we play our part in hastening the victory which we all want and of which we shall ever be proud.

Brigadier.

In the Fd.
11 May 1944.

Order of the Day, 11 May, 1944

128

he led his fearsome Goums to make a very successful attack on Mount Cairo thus enabling the final assault on Monte Cassino by the Poles who captured it on the 18th May 1944.

After being relieved by the French we went into reserve and training during which time we received our new armoured cars and White half tracks, some of the latter being equipped with 75mm guns. We thus acquired our own self propelled artillery battery of six guns.

Rome was occupied by the Allies on 4th June, two days before the Allied landings in Normandy. In the meantime 56 Division had been withdrawn to Egypt to refit. 44 Recce did not withdraw to Egypt until a little later. In the meantime we had the opportunity to visit Rome and to attend a soldiers' audience with Pope Pius XII at the Vatican. I was privileged to sit at the feet of his Holiness and found him to be very simple and dignified. We chatted about England which he knew well as he had previously been the Papal Nuncio to Britain.

In June it was now our turn to go to Egypt for rest and training. For the voyage to Egypt I was detailed with my squadron to proceed to the South of the country to Taranto to pick up two thousand German prisoners of war and transport them by ship to Alexandria. Together with a few extra troops I had about a hundred and twenty men, plus my officers, to guard them on this trip and safely deliver them to a prisoner of war camp in Egypt. We also had a number of German officer prisoners and allowed them to have some freedom aboard but on parole on the understanding they did not communicate with their soldiers. They respected this order which was convenient and avoided having to place them under guard.

The prisoners were from German units which had fought so well at Monte Cassino. They were tough and determined to make themselves difficult which they certainly did. The ship was overcrowded making it necessary to organise them into three groups. Whilst one group had their meals, another would have access to exercise on deck whilst the third were confined to their sleeping quarters. They did their best to try to disorganise this system. There was an incident when they accused us of breaking the Geneva Convention by giving them inferior bread to eat because it was white from which all goodness had been extracted. We had to convince them we fed our own troops with this lovely white bread and that under the Geneva Convention we were obliged to provide them with the same food as our own men.

After a few days at sea, we arrived and docked at Alexandria. We remained on board for the night but when we were about to disembark the following morning two prisoners were found to be missing. They had slid down the ropes to escape to an island. Fortunately they were picked up by some Egyptians and brought back on board. We then, in accordance with the Kings Army Regulations, had to hold a Court of Inquiry. The two prisoners who appeared before the Inquiry were without boots as they had discarded them on escaping. So, again invoking the Geneva Convention, they refused to cooperate unless we provided them with boots, not something normally available for this type of situation, but somehow we managed. I was relieved when later that day we handed over the required number, signed for by the prison camp commander. We returned to Italy in July 1944.

Return to British Eighth Army
(July 1944 - December 1945)

On our return from Egypt, in July 1944, 56 Division had left the American Fifth Army to rejoin the British Eighth Army, in the centre of the Apennine mountainous area in preparation for the final battles to breach the Gothic Line. This line had been well prepared by the Germans. It stretched from along the continuous mountain range from near Massa on the western coast, north of Florence, south of Bologna, across to the eastern coast to north of Ravenna. However, before reaching this line it was necessary to break through other defensive lines on the way. 44 Recce came back into operation in the area of Terni north of Rome.

On his promotion Lieutenant-Colonel Hicks was succeeded by Lieutenant-Colonel A. A. (Archie) Little, a cavalry officer from the Royals and Blues, a regiment of the Household Cavalry. It was also about this time I was promoted to become second-in-command of 44 Recce.

For a time the weather was good and we were operating in pleasant country conditions, keeping in contact with the enemy, patrolling with our scout cars and able to put our newly acquired battery of 75mm guns, under the command of Captain Bill Hammond, to good use. We were billeted in well-built sturdy farmhouses and the local population were helpful and welcoming. It was a fairly prosperous farming area. We were able to supplement our rations with the odd guinea fowl, eggs and ham, and wine which we purchased from them. The Front gradually moved on and the terrain became more difficult as we moved further into the hills where the fighting became much tougher.

Nevertheless after Perugia and Assisi had been taken I was able to visit these magnificent cities. Unlike much of Italy, these towns had not been badly damaged. The monks at the Franciscan Basilica of Saint Francis in Assisi were very welcoming and even allowed our Padre, Captain Rev. Jack Sexton, to play their organ. He played 'Ilkley Moor' among other more serious pieces. The monks seemed to enjoy the impromptu concert.

We were engaged in a number of skirmishes one of which was to capture a village atop a steep hill. The attack was made by A Squadron under command of Major Peter Osmond. Together with Archie we were witness to the failure of this attack. At first Peter advanced well up the road into this village but the Germans were there and held their fire until it was too late for the squadron to withdraw. A Squadron received a number of casualties including Peter, our well loved and very gallant South African.

In the summer of 1944 the Allied Command finally revived Operation Anvil, the planned invasion of southern France to draw off German divisions from the Normandy battle. It was originally to have been staged before the Normandy landings in June, but for several reasons was delayed. When Anvil was launched on 15th August 1944, there was a serious impact on operations in Italy. Seven of the best divisions were withdrawn, four American and three French, as well as half the Allied air forces. This was a blow to Alexander's ambition to break through the Gothic Line, and to cause the collapse of German resistance in Italy before the onset of the Italian winter. The departure of the French divisions, men particularly experienced in fighting in the mountains, was a severe handicap.

The loss of these divisions was partially made up from new units such as the first All Black American division, a Brazilian division, a Greek Brigade, and a Jewish Brigade, as well as scraping the barrel for spare troops in various parts of the Central Mediterranean theatre.

Most of them were as yet untried compared with the highly experienced troops sent to take part in Anvil. In the meantime the Germans had received substantial reinforcements to the extent that they were for a time superior in numbers to the Allied armies in Italy. It was not therefore possible to make the breakthrough before winter, which was particularly severe that year. It turned out to be one of the most difficult and toughest periods of the Italian Campaign.

Throughout September the Regiment was involved in many actions under the command of 56 Division, making attacks on the Battle for Gemmano and suffering a number of casualties. By this time the weather had deteriorated and heavy rain set in. We spent a great deal of time acting as infantry in the hills holding sectors for many weeks at a time with two squadrons up and one in reserve rotating them every week. Up in the hills it was not possible to bring up our rations on wheeled transport. We had to wait until after dark for mules to bring up our evening meal. We much looked forward to the containers of hot bully beef stew and became very anxious when they were late in arriving. During the day we ate our hard rations.

It was a period of patrols and much mortaring and shelling. We were also subjected to rocket attacks from Nebelwerfers. These are multi-tube rocket launchers; the rockets made a somewhat bloodcurdling noise on their way. Mortaring, shelling and rockets were fairly sporadic most of the time and more of a nuisance value. Nevertheless it is quite unnerving when the odd shell falls because one is always wondering when the next will arrive, as opposed to a good stonking (artillery barrage) which generally does not last long. With Archie I had quite a lot of the latter in my role as second in command, when I would come up to tactical headquarters in the early morning to be briefed by the Colonel on the day's situation. Archie seemed to have no fear and would take me somewhere in full view of the enemy and open up his maps, which very quickly attracted attention resulting in a barrage of shells. He seemed to enjoy that, whereas I just pretended I did.

In fact it was not long before Archie was killed when visiting one of the squadrons. He died a very brave man. I wrote to his mother to tell her so and received a most charming letter from her thanking me, adding that she knew 'Archie would have died as fearlessly as he rode to hounds'. On his death I immediately advised Divisional Headquarters that I had taken over command of the Regiment.

In the meantime in October after some weeks of slogging away in the hills we were given a respite in reserve and rest at Treia, a delightful hilltop town. It was like an opera setting, the town square overlooking the countryside below. Around the square was the inevitable church, the opera house, and the Marquessa's house. The soldiers were billeted in the surrounding houses whilst the officers were billeted in the house of the Marquessa herself — a charming elderly aristocratic lady who spoke no English, so we had to do our best with our pidgin French as a common language. We were some weeks in this delightful place. It does not take long before soldiers fraternise with the locals; we had quite a job to dissuade several who wanted to marry their newly acquired girlfriends.

One Sunday we planned to hold a church parade on the square and march smartly to the church for our service. The local priest was happy for us to do so but orders came down from headquarters forbidding it, as someone had complained to the Vatican.

After this rather pleasant respite we moved forward again, still under my command. On the way we were ordered to check the State of San Marino for the presence of any Germans. It had been suspected that there were German observation officers in this unique Republic in the mountains of Italy, from where they could observe the surrounding countryside towards the coast. In fact there were none but the inhabitants were delighted to see us.

The British 8th Army had advanced up the Adriatic coast into the mountains on the eastern side of the country whilst the American Fifth Army had advanced into the mountains from the west. Both armies were making slow progress in the difficult terrain in appalling weather conditions. We were again operating as infantry much of the time. In mid-November the Regiment moved to the Forli area where we had numerous close skirmishes with the enemy. We were relieved in December to return to Cesena, but it was not long before we were back into action around Faenza. Around this time Colonel Charles Spencer, from the 12th Lancers, was appointed to be our new commanding officer, so after several weeks in temporary command I resumed my role as second-in-command. As with Archie I got on very well with Charles Spencer and am very grateful for the confidence they both placed in me.

At the end of the year the Regiment went into action along the Naviglio canal and in January 1945 we had a very unpleasant spell along the river Senio. We held long stretches of the line through rain and snow, spending as much as five weeks in action at a time, subject to constant raids, shelling and rockets. We held on well with active patrolling and throwing back as many shells as our ammunition supply would allow. At the beginning of February the Germans staged an attack on our forward positions, which we managed to beat back, inflicting heavy casualties. We were relieved in mid-February and moved back for a rest across the river Lamone. Our rest was short-lived as we were back again on 3rd March to relieve an infantry battalion near Cotignola. Later that month we returned to the rear for rest and re-equipment. About this time Colonel Spencer left for leave in the U.K. so once again I assumed temporary command of the Regiment.

Our next task, together with the 12th Lancers, was to form Recforce, commanded by the colonel of the Lancers, Charles

Italy, 1944 - l to r -Capt 'Red' Milburn, Captain John Langston, self

Muddy conditions, Italy, winter 1944 - Preparing tracks for vehicles

Headquarters Squadron officers, Italy, winter 1944

Capt. Cheshire, self, Capt John Langston with adopted dog 'Io'

Spencer's old regiment. This front was a long line of defended forward positions on the Old Lamone river bed. It turned out to be a fairly quiet front. The Cheshire Regiment relieved the 12th Lancers so Recforce was renamed Checkforce.

In early April 1945, one of the infantry brigades attacked across the Reno river. To draw the enemy's attention from the main attack 44 Recce staged a simulated, or Chinese attack, putting our 75mm guns to good effect, firing off several hundred rounds of shells as well as heavy mortar and machine gun fire. By mid-April the Germans withdrew from the area and Checkforce disbanded. Elsewhere the battle was in full swing with the Germans being pushed back from the river Senio. The situation became more fluid as 56 Division advanced, whilst 44 Recce protected the division's right flank by taking over positions on Lake Comachio. We later handed this position over to an Italian unit. It was quite a terrifying experience, as we had arranged for them to take over at night. They would open fire in all directions at the slightest noise. We were lucky to get out without any friendly fire casualties.

Colonel Spencer returned from leave in April to resume command whilst I reverted to second-in-command once more. However, it was not long before he was posted to another appointment in England; this enabled me to take over command permanently, until the Regiment was disbanded in December 1945. I received immediate promotion to Lieutenant-Colonel as my two previous periods of temporary command qualified me for this rank.

German resistance by now was weakening apart from a few small engagements in which prisoners were taken. We advanced to Ferrara and finally crossed the river Po about 26th April 1945. On 29th April we crossed the river Adige. By then German resistance had almost ceased; we were then engaged in a race to be first to reach Venice. Although we were frequently held up, owing to the blowing up of bridges, my recollection is that we were ordered to stop before Venice, as the High Command had given General Freyberg, V. C., and his New Zealand troops, the privilege to enter Venice first.

I have read another account which suggested that a British infantry brigade won the race. Whichever is correct we were very disappointed and had to be content to spend the night at a beautiful villa with peacocks on the lawns at Mestre, the port and industrial area of Venice. The next day we moved on to settle in Trieste. There was little further action until hostilities in Italy ceased on 2nd May 1945.

Winding Down (May 1945 to December 1945)

The Allies had blown up all the bridges across the wide river Po which consequently seriously handicapped the Germans ability to reinforce their troops in the final battles before being forced to retreat back across the Po. Unable to bring back much of their guns and equipment they abandoned them, including hundreds of horses. Regiments quickly acquired many of these horses. It was not long before horse races were organised, including an improvised tote. We acquired a few horses ourselves, and I also picked up a small Hanomag staff car. We took these along with us to Trieste. From Trieste our role was to patrol the Italo-Yugoslav border. Marshall Tito, the Yugoslav dictator, no doubt encouraged by his Russian friends, had ambitions to annex the province of Istria including Trieste, an important Italian port for Austria and central Europe.

After several years of fighting in active warfare this new role was not too arduous. It gave us ample opportunity to ride our horses in the hilly stone wall countryside around Trieste. It was also a period when we were able to go on home leave by army lorry through Austria, Germany and France. Of course I took advantage of this and spent ten days at home with my family. We were all delighted to see each other again and the last remaining bottle of champagne, from the case I had sent home from France before the war, was opened in celebration. It was great to be back home but in many ways I found it strange. I was quite pleased when I had to return to the military life to which I had become accustomed since 1939.

During my leave in England I contacted my company Gestetner with a view to possible re-employment after the war. They were sympathetic and said they would look for something, but suggested that I stay on in the Army as I had done so well. This was not an option for me, as I knew that I would have to revert from my war rank as Lieutenant-Colonel to Lieutenant, and then train to become a regular professional soldier. A few of my more ardent officers did opt to stay in the Army and subsequently campaigned in various other theatres such as the Korean War, where one of my late squadron commanders was rewarded with an M.C.

I also took the opportunity to take some local leave and drive to Milan in my captured Hanomag for a few days, together with Major Bill Hammond, who was now my second-in-command. We met up with Signor Senti, the manager of the Gestetner Italian subsidiary. Together with his family they gave us a marvellous reception. We also spent time on Lake Garda.

Whilst the war had finished for us on 2nd May, the war in Europe did not end until VE-Day 8th, May 1945. However the war in the Far East continued until Japan surrendered on 15th August, VJ-Day, following on the successive atomic bombing of Hiroshima and Nagasaki on 6th and 9th August respectively.

In preparation for demobilisation and return to civilian life, the Army Education Corps was expanded in order to organise training programmes for all ranks and help prepare them for civilian life in various professions and trades. An education officer was allocated to each regiment for this purpose to propose courses. It soon became evident that the majority of these gentlemen had left-wing socialist ambitions. I am not alone in believing they very much influenced the 'army vote' for the General Election held on 5th July 1945 when Churchill's government was thoroughly beaten in favour of Clement Attlee. This was the only time I ever voted in a British parliamentary election, by giving a

Officers' Mess, Trieste, Dec. 1945

144

Sergeants' Mess, Trieste, Dec.1945

Lieutenant Colonel, 44 Recce 1945

ALLIED FORCE HEADQUARTERS
APO 512

23 October 1945

ORDER OF THE DAY

On parting from you, I wish it were possible to shake the hand of each of you and, in person, to say goodbye and wish you good luck.

While this method is inadequate, I cannot leave without telling you how sincerely I appreciate everything that all of you have done in the Mediterranean Theater.

Before long most of you will be home, returned to the pursuits of peace. We fought this long and terrible war to preserve and strengthen our ways of peaceful living. In all the days to come you can be proud of your contribution.

By our victory we have won great opportunities for ourselves and for the generations to follow us. We have it within our means to keep the world at peace. We can — and will — do it if we apply to the future the same spirit of understanding and cooperation which guided us during our successful struggle against the enemy.

In war all our efforts, in each of the United Nations, were concentrated toward one end — victory. In peace, all our efforts should be concentrated toward one end — a harmonious world. In such a world, freed of fears and doubts, there is no limit to human accomplishments. All of us know these things, of course, but each of us needs to repeat them again and again. Peace is worth all our efforts, and we should be alert always to preserve it.

I take leave of you with my heart full of pride for the privilege of having been associated with you of many nations in the Mediterranean Theater. You have been partners in an unbeatable team. You wrote pages of history that will never dim.

Goodbye and good luck to you all!

JOSEPH T. MCNARNEY
General, U. S. Army
Acting Supreme Allied Commander, Mediterranean Theater

Order of the Day, 23 October, 1945

147

proxy for my father to vote on my behalf. As I subsequently left to live overseas I was automatically deprived of a right to vote in the U.K.

At the end of December 1945 it was the turn of 44th Reconnaissance Regiment to be disbanded. Our 56th Divisional Commander, Major-General J Y Whitfield, C.B., D.S.O., C.B.E., came to visit to thank and congratulate us for our contribution to the Division's success during the campaign. He then took the salute as the Regiment marched past for the last time at the Trieste football stadium.

It was a sad occasion for us all as we had been together since we left Scotland in May 1942. I was proud to be a part of this fine Regiment which had unfortunately suffered losses of nearly 200 officers and other ranks killed in action from September 1942 to May 1945.

Members of the Regiment were rewarded with one C.B.E., one D.S.O., one D.C.M., five M.C., 12 M.M., one M.B.E., and 39 M.I.D.

Final Parade 44 Recce. Dec 1945. Major-General J. Y. Whitfield C.B., D.S.O., C.B.E.

44 Recce - Inspection & March Past final Parade before disbandment at Trieste December 1945. Major-General Whitfield addressing the Regiment (below, with self on left).

44 Recce - Inspection & March Past final Parade before disbandment at Trieste December 1945. Major-General Whitfield (below) taking the salute

44 Recce - Inspection & March Past final Parade before disbandment at Trieste December 1945

Skiing in Cortina d'Ampezzo, 1946. Aldo, Moira and self.

Cortina d'Ampezzo (January 1946 to March 1946)

I still had three months to go before it was my time to be demobilised. To fill in the time I was given a very pleasant assignment. With a fellow officer, Major Eric Knight, we were appointed to be responsible for running the British Military rest area at Cortina d'Ampezzo, the famous Italian ski resort in the Dolomites. The local hotels had been requisitioned to accommodate various elements of the armed forces, such as the Army, Navy and Air Force, the Polish army and others, each being allotted their respective hotels. Our job was mainly settling differences between the hotel proprietors and their respective occupants. All damages had to be properly assessed and reported on the appropriate forms to the Allied Military Government Claims and Hirings Department and referred to Area Headquarters to whom we reported in Venice. We had an office in Cortina, and a charming Italian interpreter, Aldo Bertozzi.

Life was fairly easy. I lived in a villa, which used to belong to one of the Italian noble families, with two Italian servants, a Jeep, a 15 cwt army truck as well and a rather worn out Buick staff car. Aldo, the son of the owner of the largest hotel in Cortina, became a friend and skiing instructor. We did a lot of skiing in this most delightful area in the Italian Alps. There was much partying too. Our favourite was the Polish rest hotel run by a beautiful Polish lady, Hanka Adamska.

Cortina is in the Tyrol country and part of the Belluno province of Italy. Most of the area had at one time been a part of Austria. Outside Cortina, and the principal towns, the people, language and way of life were typically Austrian Tyrolean. After the war they were agitating for the area to be returned to Austria. A part of our job was to keep an eye on this problem. I would often drive from Cortina to Venice to visit this beautiful city and its sites, paying my occasional respects to my superiors at HQ. There was always a private motor launch to take me wherever I wanted to go.

Alas, at the end of March 1946, the time had come for me to say good-bye to all my friends in Cortina d'Ampezzo to return home to face the future. The way home was by army lorry through Austria, Germany and France to Calais. This took a few days with stops for the night at army staging posts on the way.

In England I was directed to an army demobilisation centre and issued with a set of civilian clothing and ration coupons for a month. There was not a great choice of clothing so it was not uncommon to see many obviously demobilised soldiers wearing similar attire as oneself. I was now discharged with the rank of Honorary Lieutenant-Colonel and was on leave in reserve to be recalled if necessary.

I finished my military career at the age of twenty-eight after six years of active service. As an officer one is ever conscious of one's responsibility for the lives and well being of the officers and men under one's command. A battle cannot be won without the highest good morale. This can sometimes be difficult when soldiers have been separated from their loved ones at home after several years' absence, and when they have seen so many comrades pay the supreme sacrifice.

Writing letters to next of kin was always a sad duty. The replies I received were generally very appreciative and invariably very moving. Whenever possible I would try to visit the wounded, many of whom sadly never recovered, in hospital. Poignant moments.

Other Military Matters

I cannot remember exactly when it was, sometime in 1944, that I was sent to Naples to be President of a Court Marshall to try deserters, and cases of rape. This was quite an experience for a twenty-six year old Major who had had no previous legal training. As a senior officer I was appointed President of the Court together with two junior officers with the rank of Captain. We were assisted by an experienced army lawyer from the Judge Advocate-General Department, or JAG. The JAG's role was to explain and see we kept to the proper procedure in accordance with King's Regulations, the bible regulating army discipline and procedures. When the prisoner was marched into the court the JAG would read out the charge against the accused, then witnesses would be called, as the trial proceeded. The JAG would monitor the proceedings and sum up the case but on no account give an opinion on the guilt, or otherwise, of the accused. We were the judges and also had to pronounce any sentence.

I had several days of this, judging many cases in a day. If we found the accused to be guilty his previous army record would be recalled which was a help to decide the sentence. Unfortunately many had had exemplary careers up till then but had been overcome by the stress of continuous action. Nevertheless desertion in the face of the enemy was a very serious crime and merited sentences from a minimum of ten up to a maximum of twenty years. Rape, too, was also a major crime: more difficult to judge but if found guilty attracted a life sentence. These sentences under military rule

Lieutenant George Bennett and Captain Dr. Charlie Brown, 1944

were served in the 'glass house' or Army Prison Service. I understand all such sentences were sooner or later rescinded after the war.

Venereal Disease was a big problem for the army. Fraternising with the local female population was discouraged but inevitably took place. VD became such a problem that the division periodically published VD statistics by unit. I am pleased to say that 44 Recce generally had a low rate. This, I am certain, was owing to the efforts we made to occupy the troops when in periods out of action. We set up canteens and bought wine to sell to the troops. A drink or two in congenial company kept minds off other things. This applied to officers as much as to the men. Many, as I did, chose drink rather than sex. This did not imply we organised drunken orgies, although a little drunkenness did occur on occasions.

We also organised as much sport as possible — football, athletics, and various games. One of the responsibilities of a second-in-command of a regiment is to be President of the Regimental Institute, or PRI. All regiments had a PRI who held the regimental funds which were accountable to higher authority. These funds were mostly fed from profits from the sale of wine or other comforts which could be purchased through the NAAFI, or from local sources. Thus we were able to buy football and other equipment, radios, and other attractive items which were on offer through these and army channels. When I was second-in-command and therefore PRI I had a slight flair for this and am proud to say 44 Recce was among the best equipped regiments in the Corps. All squadrons could field fully equipped football teams with their own distinctive jerseys and shorts, socks and boots. We were proud of our regimental team, which won the Corps football championship in their regimental colours.

Drink reminds me of an incident early on in the campaign when my squadron was settling down for the night during a most violent thunderstorm. I have rarely seen such intense

R.S.M. Lowder

lightning, or rain, as that night. The squadron Sergeant-Major reported to me saying 'Sir, the men are drenched and cold and miserable, may I have your permission to issue them a tot of rum?'

'Sergeant-Major,' I replied, 'I did not know we had any rum.'

'Yes Sir, we have, and it is available for just this sort of situation.'

'Well, then, go ahead, Sergeant-Major!'

The squadron's keg of rum was duly produced and every one received a small tot and felt much warmer. However anything consumed in the army, used, lost, or stolen has to be accounted for and an indent made on the quartermaster for a replacement. Valuable and small items such as pistols, binoculars, or compasses require to be adequately accounted for and this includes a little keg of rum.

Soon a message came down from the higher echelons which in so many words said 'Who the hell is this Major Longley who has taken upon himself to authorise an issue of rum without reason or permission?' Such are the crimes of inexperienced wartime officers who ought to know better that rum can only be issued in times of dire and desperate necessity in time of battle. I received a mild rebuke from the Colonel, Ken Hicks, as he smilingly said 'you have committed an unforgivable military crime. Keep off the rum'.

Feminine company was fairly rare but from time to time when on leave one did have the opportunity to see and to meet members of the opposite sex, such as those in the nursing services, or driving high ranking officers around, as well as those from theatre and entertainment troupes who came from the U.K. There were voluntary organisations which sent out ladies to run canteens as well as N.A.A.F.I. staff.

Bill Hammond's sister was a nurse at one of the Army hospitals and was always a delight to meet whenever the opportunity arose. For a time we had a delightful young war correspondent, Susan Fesq (and her little dog), attached to us. I do not remember if she wrote much about us. In

Lt. Jimmy Brown, Major W.B. Hammond, Captain Peter Oldland, self, and a visit from War Correspondent, Susan Fesq, 1945

fact my experience with war correspondents was that their coverage was often very inexact, but I would not hold that against Susan. In the course of writing these memoirs I have discovered that Susan was in fact better known as Suzanne Fesq, and that after the war she became the Duchess of St. Albans.

At some time in early 1945 Ottobono Scribani-Rossi, an Italian Army officer, joined us as an interpreter. He was a very courteous and aristocratic person to have with us. He was a native of Modena, from where Balsamic vinegar comes, although I do not think he had anything to do with that condiment. He became a good friend and I corresponded with him for many years after the war.

Soldiers have a habit of using bad language, the 'F...word' being the most common expletive. It becomes very boring, rendering conversation most uninteresting when uttered practically every other word. It got so bad it started to irritate me so I quietly made it known that I hoped it might be employed in moderation. To my surprise it was quite a success and 'f...ing' was reduced to a more acceptable level.

***

It was great to be home again and to catch up with family news. As our house in Beckenham had been badly damaged my father gave it to my elder brother, Charles and his family. With the help of war damage compensation Charles converted the house into three flats. His family occupied the ground floor and the two upper floors were let. Dennis had been discharged from the Royal Air Force and started training to be a farmer to take over the Breach Farm, which had by then become our family home on the death of my grandfather during the war. It was not until many years later that Dennis was permitted to tell us he had served at Bletchley Park during the war — Bletchley Park, centre of code breaking German messages sent through the famous

'Enigma' machines, was one of the best kept wartime secrets, despite the many hundreds who served there and never gave the game away.

Charles continued to work in the family businesses in Smithfield from which my father had retired, disgusted with the heavy taxation imposed by the Socialist government under Clement Attlee. The policy of high taxation eventually destroyed many small businesses which in turn seriously affected the fortunes of the so-called middle classes. In exchange the nation gained an effective National Health Service resulting from the Beveridge Plan elaborated during the war. Industries and companies were also nationalised — not always, as it turned out, successfully. Much later Dr. Richard Beeching was called in to nationalise and reorganise the British railway system by closing hundreds of miles of secondary lines and stations.

Whilst I was still in Italy waiting for demobilisation Gestetner contacted me to offer me the position as Secretary to the Indian subsidiary. I was not happy about that as I had been away from home for so long during the war. Fortunately the offer was withdrawn before I could give an answer. I was then asked to join the French subsidiary to help in its reorganisation after the war. I accepted this assignment on the understanding that it was only temporary. As it turned out I spent the rest of my career with the French Company and still continue to live in France on retirement.

Back to Civilian Life and Gestetner

Adjusting to civilian life after nearly four years overseas was not easy, but at least I had something to which I could look forward, and was thereby able to make the adjustment without too much trauma. In many ways I was pleased to leave home, as after the initial joy I soon began to realise one's loved ones have their own lives and occupations. Although not strictly the case, I did sometimes have the sensation that I did not belong to being at home anymore, so was happy with the prospect of now facing the next chapter of my life.

On the 1st May 1946 I arrived in Paris by boat and train. A room had been booked for me at the Hotel Quai d'Orsay, a grand station hotel in the past but now rather run down. The room was comfortable and the restaurant acceptable.

I will always remember my arrival at the Gare du Nord. The 1st May in France is a national holiday so there were no porters nor taxis available; I had to lug my baggage from the station to the hotel across the Seine on a very beautiful but very hot day. I arrived in a sweat. The Manager of the French Company, Henri Bercovitch, came to welcome me and took me out for a meal at one of the large café-restaurants on the Champs Elysées. We had a chat on what he wanted me to do. Briefly he was anxious that I should do my best to help in the re-organisation of the business, at the same time ignoring all the stories I would hear about the various differences between the employees on their conduct during the wartime period. Employees who had been either in hiding in France, or in prison camps in Germany, or in Germany as 'guest' workers during the conflict, were coming back to the company. There were also those who were considered to have collaborated with the enemy. I was neutral territory and to some extent held in veneration as I had served with the victorious armies and attained the impressive rank of Lieutenant-Colonel at a relatively early age.

Henri Bercovitch was already well known to me, as I had met him in Belgium before the war, when he was managing the Belgian company. As he was Jewish and held Monegasque citizenship he was able to retire to the Principality to avoid capture by the Nazis during the war. He was a rather strange and aloof character and a heavy smoker of Boyard French cigarettes. He was very ambitious and took many risks with the pricing, and import licensing authorities, and had many other creative ideas to obtain goods to sell in order to establish a strong trading situation for the business, in which he succeeded.

General de Gaulle set up the Provisional Government in 1944 when he returned to France to organise a referendum to establish the Fourth Republic. He was President of the Provisional Government until Vincent Auriol became the first President of the Fourth Republic in 1947. René Coty was elected to succeed him in 1954.

France, like all European countries, was trying to come to terms with the aftermath of war and the occupation. The country was in a very poor state, both financially and structurally. The roads, railways, power stations and power lines were very much out of date and had suffered severely. Everything was rationed and there were frequent power cuts. Meals were restricted in restaurants to three types of menu prices, the very simple, the slightly better, and the so-called deluxe. The deluxe was a pretty poor meal just the same. However if you knew somebody who knew where to go, it was possible to have a fairly respectable 'black market' meal. Being a newcomer to France I found myself at the end of the cigarette ration queue and only able to obtain an occasional packet of *Elégantes* cigarettes, the worst of anything available. Naturally bread, meat, butter and many other essential items were on ration.

Although I was lonely and homesick for a time I soon adjusted to my new life. My first priority was to learn to speak French as I had never mastered this language in my schooldays, nor had much opportunity to practice it when I was travelling pre-war as an auditor, since all our work then was conducted in English. I took French lessons at the Berlitz school in Paris during the evenings.

I got on well with my new colleagues in the Paris office, and that of course was a great help with the language. I worked very closely with the Company Secretary, Monsieur Georges Roy, who was most kind and helpful and who taught me a great deal, not only French but about the business. I am greatly indebted to him. Another was George Girling, an Englishman, who was the buyer and in charge of all the purchasing, stores and distribution of goods. Both he and his wife were also of great help and encouragement. Girling had been working with the French company for many years before the war and had returned to England to work with Gestetner in Liverpool during the war.

All foreigners working in France were required to have a work permit in addition to a residence permit. Providing one had a work permit, or another valid reason for living in France, residence permits were fairly easy to obtain from the local Préfecture. They were renewable every three months. After a time one became entitled to a yearly permit, and eventually if you had not found fault with the authorities and your record was clean, you were granted a ten-year permit. Work permits were more difficult as priority had to be given to French nationals. Under the guise of being a technical expert, which I was not, I managed to obtain this document which also allowed me to be regularly employed and therefore entitled to the benefits of the French social security and health services.

The chairman of the French Company was Monsieur André Augis, a jovial Frenchman, a connoisseur of fine wines, who knew all the best restaurants. Although not a practising lawyer himself, he was pre-war a pioneer in the profession of legal advisor. He spoke excellent English and was chairman of many subsidiaries of foreign companies. He had survived the war in good relationship with the German occupation authorities without becoming alienated from the overseas owners of these companies. He was much involved with the Germans in safeguarding the interests of foreign companies. The Germans did not interfere with the management of the French Company, except of course to ensure the company complied with German army and civil directives. This naturally also ensured priority to supply them with Gestetner goods, some of which were now being made in France. A German business administrator occupied an office in our premises from which he similarly supervised several other businesses. He was apparently a very charming person and was generally well liked. Surprisingly a royalty agreement was drawn up between the Company and the German and French authorities by which royalties should be set aside to remunerate the parent Company for any goods produced in France under the Gestetner name during the occupation. These monies were regularly remitted to a blocked bank account in France in favour of Gestetner Ltd, London. The Germans presumably were looking forward to using this cash to develop the Gestetner business in the U.K. when they had won the war. As they failed to achieve that goal, the accumulated royalties had become quite a significant amount, which was immediately available for transfer to London after the war. Without a hitch and much to the parent company's delight the French monetary authorities gave permission for this transfer. It was a fine example of German thoroughness as well as André Augis' foresight in arranging for the royalty agreement.

Another important personality of the Company was the sales manager for Paris, Monsieur Emile Valentin. He got on well with the German overseer, at the same time playing a very good double role in managing to hide, or arrange, for young male employees to avoid being drafted to Germany as 'guest' workers. He was also instrumental in saving several Jewish employees from being sent to prison camps. I met many who owed a great deal to Emile Valentin for the risks he took on their behalf.

During the occupation it was not easy to find raw materials to manufacture new duplicators and to restore old ones. Likewise for the manufacture of stencils, inks, and other accessories as well as sourcing suitable paper for the duplicating process. Most of the company's local production was commandeered by the Germans, who also monitored a minimum supply to French customers, mainly for use by French government offices, and other officially recognised organisations. However, the underground movement managed to find access to duplicators, their supplies and papers, in order to print and distribute clandestine newspapers and propaganda for the resistance movement.

The chairman, André Augis, together with Fritz Kung (wartime manager of the French Company, a German speaking Swiss and a former member of the Company's continental audit staff) and Abel Ticon (wartime manager of the Gestetner branches in the unoccupied zone) had acquired a small factory in the Paris suburb of Rueil Malmaison, the Manufacture Française d'Appareils Duplicateurs et de Stencils, which manufactured stencils and inks. As they had bought this business in their own names the parent company in London compelled them to sell it to the French subsidiary after the war. It was felt that both Kung and Ticon had collaborated too much with the Germans.

London felt it necessary to change the management in France, so Fritz Kung was transferred to manage the smaller Belgian subsidiary. He was succeeded by Henri Bercovitch shortly before I arrived in France. Abel Ticon was eventually sacked as he was not prepared to abandon his role as wartime manager of the branches in the old occupied zone and revert to become simply manager of the Lyons branch.

Henri Bercovitch quite naturally was not prepared to share management of the French company with Ticon. It was in reality a case of settling scores to establish undisputed control of the business. I was despatched to Lyon to ensure Ticon's departure. He subsequently sued the Company in the Prud'homme Court for an enormous sum. The Company won the case.

In my first year in France I found it very difficult to live on my salary and had to supplement my existence by drawing on my savings. I was pleased therefore to receive a handsome bonus at the end of the year and a rise in salary. I also gave up wasting money on a hotel room and found accommodation in the rue Lauriston chez Madame Spira-Levy, who rented me a room for a modest sum. About the same time I discovered and joined the British Officers Club in the rue du Faubourg Saint Honoré, a palatial mansion next to the British Embassy residence. This club was open to the many British officers stationed in Paris, as well as ex-officers, and members of the Embassy and other British missions in Paris. It was a godsend, where meals were good and reasonable. There were well-stocked bars with drinks equally reasonably priced. It became the meeting place for the British community; it was where I met many new friends. The club premises had originally belonged to the Rothschild family and had a beautiful garden down to the Champs Elysées. On my first visit I was greeted by George Trippas, who was the 'Maître d'hôtel'. George had come to Paris many years before the war to learn to be a waiter and had served in some of the great Parisian hotels, where he met many famous people. He had been very fond of the famous French actor, Sacha Guitry, who had an apartment pre-war in an hotel where George worked. Sacha Guitry would invite George to sit down and smoke a cigarette with him whilst he recounted anecdotes about his fantastic life as an actor.

George had been interned by the Germans, spending the war in camps reserved for Britons caught in Paris when the

Germans entered the city. When the Officers Club eventually closed, George continued to work as a waiter and was well known in Paris, particularly among the British community.

I was beginning to enjoy my life in Paris, joining the Club du Jeu de Paume to play squash, and the exclusive Racing Club de France in the Bois de Boulogne to play tennis and use their excellent swimming pool. The Racing Club was within walking distance from my new home.

I made some very firm lifelong friendships with fellow members of the Officers Club, particularly Alan Harris and Digby Verdon-Roe. Alan had been a Major in the army and returned to France to study the recent French invention of pre-stressed concrete. This was a process of producing concrete structures to render them much lighter and stronger. Alan later returned to England and set up his own civil engineering business to develop the process in the U.K. and Australia. He became very well known in his profession as a civil engineer, being knighted as Professor Sir Alan Harris, C.B.E. Allan married Mathé, a French graduate of Vasser, the American woman's university college whom he met in the United States. I was Best Man at their wedding in Paris. They adopted two boys. Both he and his wife were devout Roman Catholics and lived in the shadow of Westminster Cathedral. Alan died soon after his eightieth birthday.

Digby had been an officer in the Royal Air Force; he came to France shortly after me. He was a Chartered Accountant in partnership with another British accountant in Paris. By successive amalgamations between accountancy firms he became senior partner in Paris for the firm which eventually became Ernst and Young. He married Gwyneth Roberts shortly after I married Ginette. Both girls had been working at the British Embassy. Digby was a member of the Verdon-Roe family which produced the famous Avro planes during the 1914-18 War. He retired to the U.K. and died many years ago but is survived by Gwyneth and their two daughters with whom I remain in touch.

The Silver Box

by
JOHN GALSWORTHY

presented
by

The Anglo-French Players

Under the patronage of H. E. the British Ambassador
The Rt Hon A. Duff Cooper D. S. O.

Producer
Stanley HUMBERT

Stage Manager
Gilbert CAUMONT

Scenery by
TAHAR   Jane LITHIBY
assisted by Henri MAGUY

Costumes by
GRANIER

Furniture
Mr. A. BISSEY

Anglo-French Players, Paris 1948

170

Ginette

In late 1947 I became aware of a rather attractive vivacious young girl always surrounded by many admirers and who loved to dance. As usual being rather shy, and an appalling dancer, I felt I would have very little chance of approaching this enchanting person. When I saw my good friend, Alan Harris, sweeping across the dance floor at the Officers Club with this girl in his arms, dancing a *paso doble* with great *panache* a pang of envy inspired me to pluck up courage to introduce myself. Thus I met Miss Ginette Edith Wilson, who was also a member of the British Embassy staff next door.

I do not think I impressed her with my clumsy dancing but we seemed to get on well. In fact we became very good friends when we both joined an amateur dramatic society, The Anglo-French Players, which was rehearsing 'The Silver Box', a play by John Galsworthy. The Anglo-French Players was formed by a mutual friend, Stanley Humbert, who was also a member of the Officers Club and ran a small business teaching English. Most of the members of the cast, including Ginette, were also members of the Club, enabling us all to get to know each other well. Ginette played the role of the 'Unknown Lady' whilst I was cast as 'Detective Snow'. My part was fairly minor compared with Ginette's more important major role. We had great fun. The play which was finally performed on the stage of the ballroom in the Officers Club before a distinguished audience, including the then British Ambassador, Sir Duff Cooper and his wife Lady Diana. Apart from Ginette, other members of the Embassy took part, or helped in the production. They included the Ambassador's Private Secretary, Eric, Viscount Duncannon, who later succeeded to his father's title as Lord Bessborough. Other particular friends members of the cast were Alan Harris, who took the part of John Braithwaite, M.P., and Donald Cunnynghame-Robertson the part of a Magistrate's clerk. Donald, holding a similar position to me at Gestetner, was working for ICI France and later became its Managing Director for France, whilst I was later privileged to become Managing Director of Gestetner France.

The idea of marrying Ginette was no doubt at the back of my mind when I invited her to spend part of her holidays with me in early summer of 1948, at my family's farm at Cranbrook. We travelled by train and boat to Dover. From there we took a train to Staplehurst, Kent, where my father came to meet us. The visit was a great success and Ginette instantly captivated all my family. I told them that my friendship with Ginette was not a serious affair. They did not believe me and were not surprised when a few weeks later I told them I had become engaged. My parents were delighted, particularly as they had not been very impressed with any of my girl friends up till then.

On 15th August 1948, to pluck up courage to propose to Ginette, I took her by train to Saint Nom la Brêteche, not far from Paris. I was by then very much in love with this girl and to my delight, over a very good meal, she accepted my proposal.

I then met my future parents-in-law, Albert and Germaine Wilson, as well as Ginette's sister Jacqueline and her husband Thomas Mason, M.B.E., with their baby daughter Carol. They were then all living at their family flat at Bois Colombes, a suburb of Paris. I was duly accepted in the family.

We set the date for our marriage in early January 1949 at the British Embassy Church, of which I had been a member since my arrival in Paris. The British Embassy Church in the rue d'Aguésseau, in the eighth arrondissement, is an Anglican church very near to the British Embassy. The Chaplain was Bishop Chambers, a very kindly elderly person. He was Australian by birth and had been a bishop in Tanganyika. Although the church was styled as such it was not a part of the Embassy; it did maintain a close relationship but was otherwise quite independent.

Technically an Anglican, Ginette had not been baptised but was keen to be baptised before our marriage. She wanted this to be done by the then official chaplain at the Embassy, the Reverend Dunbar. However this was not possible at the British Embassy Church as Bishop Chambers and the Embassy chaplain were in disagreement with each other. The baptism took place at the American Episcopal Cathedral of Paris in the Avenue George V. The reasons for this difference I did not know, but the Embassy chaplain, although well liked by the Embassy staff, was to my mind quite an odd person.

Ginette's parents had met in France during the Great War, when Albert Wilson was a soldier in the British Army. He joined as a private soldier and saw active service in the line, being promoted to sergeant, a rank he lost through gambling at cards. He met Germaine Dalmar when on leave in Normandy. They fell in love although neither of them could speak the other's language. This did not prevent them from marrying. For a short while they lived in England after the war but soon returned to France where Albert took up employment as a bank clerk. Germaine was the daughter of a Breton family which had settled at Dives-sur-Mer in Normandy. The Dalmar family were not very wealthy.

In due course their first daughter, Jacqueline, was born at the Hertford British Hospital in Levallois-Perret, to be followed by the birth of Ginette Edith on 13th August 1922. The family eventually bought a flat in Bois Colombes where Ginette and her sister grew up and went to the local schools.

Albert worked for various banks but lost his job in the Great Depression years. He found work with the American

Express Bank. It was a very trying time for them but Germaine was a strong character and managed the family's finances capably. Albert eventually got a job as an internal auditor with the American oil company, Standard Oil of New Jersey (Esso). Except for the war years he held this employment until his retirement.

Ginette was perfectly bi-lingual and quite at ease in either language. From time to time she had stayed with her grandparents at Waltham Abbey, or with her aunt Muriel in London. Furthermore together with her father, mother and sister, she had spent the war years in England.

Before the German invasion of France in 1940 Ginette's father was auditing Esso's refineries and other installations in this country. He was working for a time at Nantes on the West coast so the family hired a house for the summer at the nearby seaside resort of La Baule. From all accounts this was a joyous time, particularly for the two teenagers. Ginette was then eighteen.

While they were there, the Germans invaded France and occupied Paris so they were unable to go back home to Bois Colombes. As the situation worsened, the British Consul at Nantes advised all British citizens to head for Bordeaux in the hope of finding a ship sailing for England. They managed to take a bus to Bordeaux, the girls taking their precious bicycles with them.

There was chaos in Bordeaux; hundreds of British nationals were trying to return to the United Kingdom. As there were no boats sailing for England from there, the Consul directed them to Le Verdon at the mouth of the Gironde River to take the 'last' boat for England. This turned out to be a small Dutch cargo carrying wood, hardly big enough to accommodate all those hundreds of people who claim to have left Bordeaux on the 'last' boat. I have met several people who claim to have been on that 'last boat' so no doubt there must have been many last boats. Much to the girls' disgust they were not permitted to embark with their bicycles so sadly were obliged to jettison them. After about a week at sea they landed at Falmouth. During the voyage the ship was bombed by German aircraft, luckily without effect. There was no accommodation for the refugees on board. They had to sleep on deck but luckily the weather was good. The ship only had a small crew who were not equipped to cater for the extra numbers. However they did their best to provide cocoa and biscuits.

On disembarkation all the passengers were directed to a cinema for the night until they had been vetted by the police and immigration authorities to prove they were not suspicious characters. Although the passengers held British passports some had no address to go to in the U.K. Luckily Ginette's family were able to call on her father's family where they went to stay for some time.

Albert Wilson with his connections with Esso managed to find a job with the Petroleum Board at Shell House in London. The Board had the responsibility to allocate petroleum products in the country. Both Ginette and her sister Jacqueline also found employment there counting petrol coupons for distribution.

The family eventually managed to buy a house at Southgate, a pleasant suburb north of London. They were very happy there and soon made firm friends with their neighbours largely thanks to Ginette's mother, Germaine, who was quite a personality with a charming accent in English, not unlike the accent of Yvonne Arnaud, a popular French actress on the London stage in those days.

During this period the situation in France had forced the French to call for an armistice which resulted in the British Army having to evacuate from Dunkirk, together with a certain number of French troops. General Charles de Gaulle left France. Following his famous broadcast appeal on 18th June 1942 calling for French men and women wherever they were to rally to his cause, he set up his Free French Force in England. There was not only a nucleus of French soldiers, sailors, and airmen, and civilians who had managed to reach the U.K, there were important French Forces in the unoccupied countries of the French Empire, many of whom rallied to de Gaulle's call.

In France Marshal Pétain was appointed head of the French government and delegated to agree surrender terms with Germany. The northern part of the country and the eastern coastal areas came under German occupation and rule; the unoccupied area of southern France was governed by Pétain's government based in Vichy.

Back in England it was not long before Ginette answered an advertisement in the British press calling for French citizens to apply to work for Général de Gaulle. Having both French and British citizenship she was quite naturally eligible to apply. Ginette was interviewed and became a member of Général de Gaulle's Cabinet Particulier (Private Office) at 4 Carlton Gardens, in London. She was employed in the 'Chiffres Section' (Telegrams). This was highly confidential work, typing and receiving telegrams, many of which were in code. As a member of de Gaulle's headquarters Ginette was not a member of the Free French Forces, a separate military organisation under de Gaulle's command.

Although she met de Gaulle on a few occasions he was not the sort of person to wander down the office for a chat. He was indeed apparently somewhat aloof. Whilst working at Carlton Gardens, Ginette came into contact and worked with many young French men who later became well known personalities, particularly after de Gaulle returned to France. For example Maurice Schuman, in charge of the press section and propaganda, later became Foreign Minister. Olivier Wormser became Governor of the Bank of France, Roger Frey became President of the Constitutional Council, Jean-Marie Paris became a Deputy in the French Parliament. Later Maurice Couve de Murville joined de Gaulle. He became a Foreign Minister and Prime Minister in later governments. They all knew each other well and at various functions in

COMITE NATIONAL FRANCAIS

SECRETARIAT GENERAL A LA COORDINATION

BUREAU DU PERSONNEL

BP/E/ 217 le 27 juillet 1942.-.......

AVIS D'ENGAGEMENT

Mademoiselle Ginette WILSON.	: est engagé dans le Personnel Civil au Comité National Français.
ADRESSE:	: 92a, Londsdale Drive, Enfield, West, Mx.
en qualité de	: dactylographe bilingue.
à partir du	: 4 juillet 1942. -
Au traitement de (Soumis aux impôts et taxes en vigueur)	: £15 par mois.
Affectation jusqu'à nouvel ordre	: Cabinet du Général de Gaulle.
Observations:	

Très important: Suivant les usages locaux, l'engagement ci-dessus est fait à titre provisoire, et peut à tout moment être rèsilié pendant la période d'essai de deux semaines.

Le Chef du Personnel Civil

FRANCE LIBRE PERSONNEL CIVIL

Destinataires:
Cabinet du Général de Gaulle.
Ct. du Q.G. Carlton Gardens.
Service de Sécurité.
Melle G. WILSON.
(2) Archives.

Ginette's employment contract for Gen. de Gaulle's Private Office, London 1942

RÉPUBLIQUE FRANCAISE

PRESTATION DE SERMENT.

Je soussignée Ginette WILSON,
du Cabinet de la Présidence, jure de ne jamais révéler,
hors le cas où j'en serais légalement requise par les
Autorités de la France Combattante, aucun fait, propos
ou écrit relatifs au Service, qui seront venus à ma con-
naissance dans le service, ou à l'occasion du service,
sous peine de renvoi immédiat sans compensation ou in-
demnité et sans préjudice de toutes sanctions que de droit.

Londres, le 30 juillet 1942.-

Signature de l'Intéressée.

Ginette Wilson

Serment prêté devant:

M. le Capitaine de frégate GALLERET,
Sous chef de l'Etat-Major Particulier,
du Général de Gaulle:

Galleret

M. le Capitaine FENART,   M. le Capitaine COULET,
Chef du Personnel Civil,   Chef de Cabinet du Général de
                                 Gaulle

                                 F. Coulet

Ginette's swearing secrecy to Général de Gaulle's cabinet

178

France over the years we would meet some of them, enabling Ginette to catch up on their news.

Général de Gaulle moved his Headquarters to Algeria in North Africa in 1943. Ginette was invited to go with them but declined. Instead she remained at Carlton Gardens which then became The French Embassy in London with René Massigli as the French Ambassador to the Court of Saint James.

During the time of the German air raids over London Ginette often had to work late. Although there was a shelter at Carlton Gardens hardly anyone used it; the General never took shelter there so his staff did not do so either. It was very scary for Ginette when she had to return home, braving the bombs as she walked to the Underground and then walking back home from the station at Southgate with shrapnel falling around. Her father, who was also an air raid warden, often used to come to meet her to escort her home.

At some time during the war when she was in the U.K, Ginette met a young Canadian airman to whom she became engaged. Sadly she had to bear the pain when he was shot down and killed.

In 1944 or early 1945 the family returned to France to reoccupy their flat in Bois Colombes where they found that much of their furniture had disappeared, taken by neighbours who had been 'looking after it' for them. They eventually recovered most of it. Ginette's father resumed his job with Standard Oil of New Jersey based in France but travelling all over the country as well to neighbouring countries as a part of the Esso audit team reporting to New York.

On her return to France, Ginette of course gave up her situation at the French Embassy in London. She then applied for a job with the British Embassy in Paris. As she did not have diplomatic status she was locally engaged as a typist. At some stage she was in charge of the Travel Section, a post she much enjoyed. Travel was difficult and often reserved for privileged travellers. All the Commonwealth Embassies as well as the different British commissions in Paris had access to this section. Many important people used their charm to obtain tickets. In fact V.I.P.s travelling to the U.K. requiring priority had to pass through the Embassy travel section. Later Ginette worked for one of the political ministers at the Embassy. On one occasion Monsieur Léon Blum, a French Socialist politician, at the time editor of the socialist newspaper *Le Populaire*, sought her help to contact someone at the Embassy to pass a note to Anthony Eden. Léon Blum went on to become France's first post war Socialist Prime Minister.

When I first met Ginette she was working as Personal Assistant to Squadron Leader 'Dickie' Graves, who had been a Battle of Britain pilot. He was number two to Air Vice-Marshal Collier, Minister for Civil Aviation at the Embassy. Dickie was a very colourful character who spent a great deal of his time partying. It sometimes seemed to me that Ginette's main job was to telephone around to try to trace Dickie after a night out when he was wanted for a meeting at the Embassy.

Sir Duff Cooper was the first British Ambassador to France after the war. Sir Duff, together with his wife Lady Diana, were a brilliant couple. Duff Cooper had been not only a gallant soldier in the First World War, and an inter-war politician, he had also been a member of the famous and fashionable circle of friends known as the Coterie. It was at this time he met the beautiful Lady Diana Manners whom he married in 1919. As Ambassador, the social centre of Parisian life was undoubtedly at the British Embassy in Paris.

The British Embassy was an exciting place to work in those days immediately after the war, particularly for a young and attractive girl of twenty-four. Christopher Soames was the young Assistant Military Attaché at the time. It was at the Embassy that he met his future wife, Mary Churchill, the youngest daughter of Winston Churchill. Ginette was invited to their wedding in London but was unable to attend. Lady Diana often arranged parties at the Embassy for John

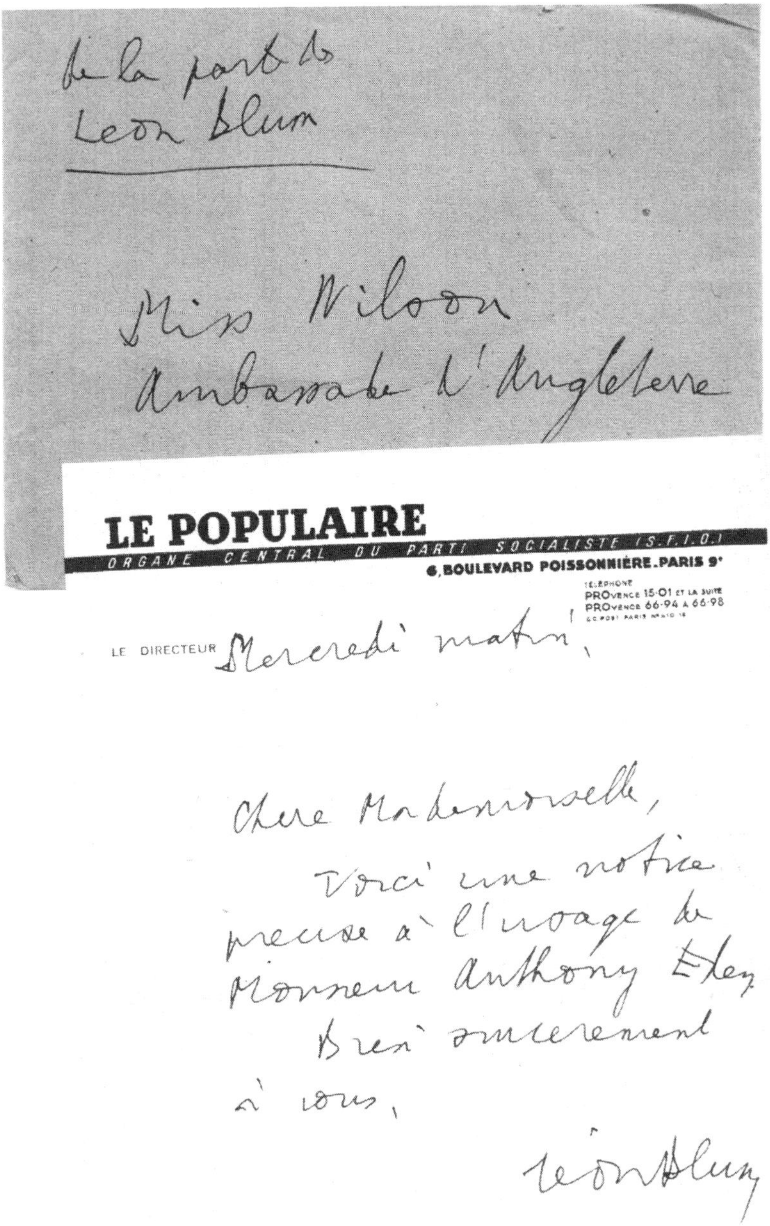
de la part de
Léon Blum

Miss Wilson
Ambassade d'Angleterre

LE POPULAIRE
ORGANE CENTRAL DU PARTI SOCIALISTE (S.F.I.O.)
6, BOULEVARD POISSONNIÈRE. PARIS 9e
TÉLÉPHONE
PROvence 15-01 et la suite
PROvence 66-94 à 66-98

LE DIRECTEUR Mercredi matin,

Chère Mademoiselle,
Voici une notice
précise à l'usage de
Monsieur Anthony Eden.
Bien sincèrement
à vous,

Léon Blum

Léon Blum's note to Ginette

Miss Wilson

MR. & MRS. CHURCHILL

REQUEST THE HONOUR OF

YOUR COMPANY

AT THE MARRIAGE OF THEIR DAUGHTER

MARY

TO

CAPTAIN CHRISTOPHER SOAMES,

COLDSTREAM GUARDS,

AT ST. MARGARET'S WESTMINSTER

ON TUESDAY, FEBRUARY THE 11TH,

AT 2.30 P.M.,

AND AFTERWARDS AT

THE DORCHESTER

(BALLROOM ENTRANCE, PARK LANE.)

PLEASE SEND AN
EARLY REPLY TO

MRS. CHURCHILL,
28, HYDE PARK GATE, S.W.7

PLEASE BRING THIS INVITATION BOTH TO
THE CHURCH AND TO THE RECEPTION.

Ginette's invitation to Mary Churchill's wedding, 1947

Julius Cooper (later Lord Norwich), Duff and Diana's son, to which Ginette would invariably be invited.

Ginette's brother-in-law Thomas (Tom) Mason, a Regimental Sergeant-Major in one of the Guards Regiments, was in charge of the office of General Sir Guy Salisbury-Jones, the Military Attaché at the Embassy. Jacqueline and Tom had married sometime before I came on the scene when Tom was serving with the British Army on the Rhine prior to his demobilisation. I believe Tom's appointment at the Embassy was due to Guy Salisbury-Jones' influence as they had known each other in the army. Guy Salisbury-Jones was a wine connoisseur and had studied the art of making wine. On his retirement he was a pioneer in setting up a vineyard in southern England — an industry which has developed steadily ever since.

Shortly after I became engaged to Ginette, her family bought a house in Avenue Gallieni in Le Vésinet in the Seine et Oise department, later to be renamed the department of Yvelines, about fifteen kilometres west of Paris. Le Vésinet is a charming suburb with fine parks, streams, and lakes. It is a listed area which used to be part of the royal hunting grounds of the nearby castle of Saint Germain-en-Laye. It was acquired for development when the royal estates were disbanded.

During our period of engagement I was quietly making my way with Gestetner in France. My French was improving and so was my remuneration. I was getting on well with my colleagues in the office. My work entailed quite a lot of travelling to the branches in France and in North Africa. Travelling in France was by train in those days and by air to Africa. On one of these tours I flew to Casablanca, where the manager was Jean-Pierre Kipfmuller. Jean-Pierre was a delightful person and we subsequently became good friends. He was a keen amateur pilot who shared a small plane with one of his friends. We had to go from Casablanca to Tangiers. Jean-Pierre invited me to go with him in his small plane together with his friend as co-pilot. This was my first

Our wedding, 15th January 1949

experience in such a small craft, in which I was tucked in a seat behind the pilots. On account of cloud we nearly had to turn back in crossing the hills between Casablanca and Tangiers. We had to make two attempts to get through but arrived safely, although there was apparently some concern as we were reported overdue.

Tangiers was a free port so the shops were bulging with every conceivable type of goods from Britain and other countries, items which were not available in France nor the United Kingdom. My friends stacked up with cigarettes whilst I bought a set of beautiful Witney wool blankets. It was not possible to bring them back with us on the plane so I had them sent to Casablanca under customs. As I had to go on later by Air France to Algiers and then to Tunis these blankets followed me all the way. Thereafter I ran into a problem. Having arrived by bus at Tunis airport with the other passengers, we were waiting to embark on our plane for Paris when its undercarriage partially collapsed before our eyes. We had to return to Tunis for the night. The following evening we returned to the airport to watch mechanics hammering at something on one of the engines. After the previous day's experience this was not very reassuring. After a few engine trials we embarked for Paris much behind schedule. At Le Bourget we passed customs but my blankets were not on the plane. A search was made for them in the customs sheds to no avail. It was getting very late. Whilst waiting, the other passengers were becoming very impatient with me for holding up the bus to take us into Paris to the airline terminal at Les Invalides. To my astonishment my blankets had arrived before me and had managed to pass customs without any formality nor duty. We have used these blankets ever since.

In the meantime Ginette and I happily pursued our engagement. We had the opportunity to exchange many loving letters during my absences from Paris. When I now read some I had written to Ginette in those days I am astonished I wrote them so well. Even my writing was legible.

Ginette

Our civil marriage took place at the Mairie (town hall) of Le Vésinet on 7th January 1949. The Maire, Monsieur Jean-Marie Louvel, then the Minister for Industry in the French Government, performed the ceremony. As is appropriate on these occasions the Maire makes a little speech pronouncing the words laid down for the occasion and presents one with the Livret de Famille. The Livret de Famille (in which is inscribed the essential information about the marriage and provides for the inscription of any future children) registers the regime under which one is married, in our case, 'Communauté de Biens'. This is the simplest and most common marriage contract which stipulates that all one's goods and chattels as well as any earnings of either party are shared in common. In the course of one's married life it is possible to change the marriage contract if the parties agree. We did this some years later to the regime of 'Communauté Universelle'. This stipulates that on the death of one of the partners the other inherits all the property without inheritance tax until the death of the survivor — the advantage being that no relatives can at that time have any claim on the estate.

If there were any children of the marriage, which was not our case, it would be necessary to obtain the agreement of the children prior to such a marriage contract. A change in a marriage contract has to be officially noted in the 'Livret de Famille'. It is a sort of family passport which one holds onto preciously for the rest of one's life. Germaine and Albert Wilson, my newly acquired parents-in-law, attended the civil marriage ceremony, as did Jacqueline and Tom Mason, my newly acquired brother- and sister-in-law. We all crossed the road after the ceremony for a drink in the local café, after which we dispersed to return home or to our respective professional occupations. A civil marriage ceremony is not a very glamorous affair, although some make it so. In our case we were due to hold our Christian marriage in church the following week. For both of us it was a bit of an anti-climax as we were now legally married but not yet married in Church.

We arranged for my family to come over from England a few days prior to our church wedding. They came together: my parents, Biddy with her husband Mark, Charles with his wife Dorothy, and Dennis who was not married in those days. Nell Coath came too. They all stayed at the Hotel du Louvre at the end of the Avenue de l'Opéra.

I arranged a dinner for both our families to meet for the first time. It was held at the restaurant of the Hotel Westminster in the Avenue de la Paix where George Trippas had become Maître d'Hôtel after leaving the Officers Club. It was a great success and George had made us all so welcome. We stayed at table until quite late and much wine was consumed with many toasts and singing. Our families had suddenly become life-long friends, much to our joy.

The following day we were invited to Le Vésinet to be dined by my in-laws. Another successful and hilarious occasion. My father-in-law had bought some wine in barrels, one of which I remember was Châteauneuf-du-Pape. He and my brother-in-law Tom had previously had spent much time in the cellar bottling this wine. On occasions they emerged quite intoxicated from the fumes in the confined space, although we suspect a refreshing glass or two may have contributed to this state of being.

Well, we managed to get to The British Embassy Church on time the following day. Ginette looked very beautiful in a lovely dress designed for her and which was based on a design by the fashion house, Christian Dior. The bridesmaids, children of Ginette's cousins, were also very pretty in their white dresses. I had obtained permission from the Military Attaché, General Sir Guy Salisbury-Jones, to wear my uniform. Among the several guests, apart from our families, I had invited several of the friends I had met at the Officers Club whilst Ginette had invited several of her chums from the Embassy. Bishop Chambers took the ceremony and made a very charming address.

We held a reception at premises in the Avenue Gabriel which had replaced the Officers Club. It all went very well and in due time we slipped away for our honeymoon at Megève, the ski resort. We travelled overnight by train which was perhaps not the most comfortable, nor most romantic way of starting married life. We had booked rooms for two weeks at the Hotel Résidence, in the centre of the town, which has since disappeared. It was very comfortable and well placed for access to the ski slopes. Good restaurant, a band and dancing in the evening. Although we had both skied before our marriage we were not very expert but had much fun on the slopes with plenty of falls and luckily no damage.

Honeymoon, Megève, 1949

Married Life

For the first eight months of our marriage we lived at my parent's-in-laws's house in Le Vésinet, during which time Ginette's parents were generally absent on their business travels. However we shared the accommodation with Jacqueline and Tom Mason and their small child, Carol. At the best of times this is not generally a very happy arrangement. Although we got on well together there were strains. Jacqueline and Tom occupied a room on the first floor whilst Ginette and I occupied a room on the second floor, and we shared the rest of the house.

It was not long before we found and purchased a small house in Le Vésinet at 67 Boulevard d'Angleterre. The price was within my budget. The vendors had built it just before the war. There was a salon and dining room and kitchen on the ground floor with three rooms upstairs and one bathroom. The garage was in the basement together with a laundry area. There was a coal-burning boiler for house heating whilst the hot water was heated by an electric water tank. There was a pleasant small garden with a waist-high cemented ornamental pool which we used as a mini-swimming pool during the summer.

After suitable redecoration we proudly took possession of our first house in October 1949, and had the fun of buying furniture and fittings, some of which we purchased in England. To start with, more or less all we had were the blankets I had bought in Tangiers.

Prior to moving into our first house I bought our first car, a Peugeot 203. Car production in France at that time had

Our first house in Le Vésinet, December 1949

... and its garden in 1986

difficulty keeping up with demand. It was thanks to the good relations of the Gestetner branch manager with the local Peugeot dealer in Rouen that I managed to secure this vehicle. We took the train to Rouen, picked up the car, and then spent the week-end at a very pleasant auberge. It was a very attractive area for me. The auberge was at a point on the Seine at Villequier where there was a pilot station; all ships sailing to and from Rouen stopped to pick up or drop off their pilot.

Villequier is famous for its association with French author, Victor Hugo. He had a house on the high ground overlooking the Seine. The great tragedy in his life was the loss of his daughter Leopoldine Vacquérie who, together with her husband, was drowned when their recently purchased yacht capsized in a sudden gust of wind in front of Victor Hugo's house. He abandoned the house in his sorrow. Owing to political differences with the Emperor Louis Napoléon he eventually went into voluntary exile on the Isle of Guernsey for nine years.

Although I was qualified to drive in France with my international driving licence, it was necessary, as I had become a resident, to pass a test to obtain a French licence, or 'permis de conduire'. Ginette also decided to take driving lessons. We both passed our driving test without any problem. This is something very rare today; it often takes a person several attempts before he or she succeeds in obtaining this all-important document, which, incidentally, is for life, unlike British driving licences which have to be renewed periodically.

We bought a Fiat 500 for Ginette to drive locally to see her parents and sister and do the local shopping. A husband is notoriously nervous when his spouse drives, and I must confess I never felt that Ginette ever developed a good road sense. This was probably unfair and certainly contributed to her lack of confidence. She never ventured much outside the confines of Le Vésinet although there were a few occasions

On holiday in Austria in 1955

when she ventured to Paris to see friends. The harrowing stories about how she missed this or that collision on account of the stupidity of the other driver did seriously concern me. Unfortunately we never developed a husband/wife driving partnership for long journeys.

From time to time my parents would come over by the London-Paris night train, or the Golden Arrow train and boat daylight service from Dover to Calais. They much enjoyed their visits when they would meet our friends. We would also discover good restaurants together. They sometimes came on holiday with us to La Baule in Britanny, or Deauville in Normandy and one hilarious visit to the Châteaux in the Loire Valley.

In those days we were all smokers, my mother outstripping the rest of us. It was during one of these visits that Ginette had a nasty bout of bronchitis, which we thought must be — and probably was — due to smoking. We had no personal doctor at the time but managed to find one. He was rather old and surprisingly did not possess a stethoscope so put his ear to Ginette's chest to listen to her heart. We thought this was very odd, but he proclaimed that Ginette's heart was behaving in a mysterious and irregular way and that she must immediately see a specialist.

As was the habit in those days among expatriates we contacted the American Hospital of Paris managing to get an appointment with Professor LeNegre, the top cardiologist of his day. His report was that, despite an irregular heart beat, there was nothing to worry about, and that she should come back to consult him in ten years time. We were comforted by this, but in later years the condition did worry various doctors as the condition got worse. It was not until the early nineteen-eighties did her current cardiologist diagnose that she suffered from obstructive cardio-myopathy, owing to a congenital malformation of the heart. Whilst this condition is not generally a great problem in the earlier years of one's life, it becomes increasingly so in later life. This was very much

Cruising, with Peter Longley (above) and Captain Ronald Warwick, Commodore of the Cunard Fleet.

Cruising in 2000; Cabin 2081 of the QE2.

the case for Ginette whose health deteriorated gradually over the years until she sadly died on 6th July 2006, aged 84. We had enjoyed a very happy and active life of fifty-seven years together. It should be noted that when we consulted Professor LeNegre this particular heart condition had not had not yet been recognised as such.

As so many of our generation, Ginette never worked again once we were married. She was able to assist me in the important social side of my career, entertaining colleagues from London and other parts of the world. She was an avid reader, perhaps preferably in English rather than French. She took up lessons in book-binding at which she became quite proficient. For a time her hobby was tapestry. Ginette had a good singing voice although she did not practice it very much. She would have liked to have been a talent spotter for popular songs and singers. In fact very often she would claim that an hitherto unknown singer or song would make the charts. Sooner or later she would invariably be proved to have made a discovery.

We travelled regularly on business and on holiday, and, after my retirement we cruised practically every year. My godson and nephew, Peter Longley, was for many years cruise director on the QE2, so we frequently cruised or crossed the Atlantic with him. Peter has many talents. With an honours degree in theology at Cambridge, he paints, writes, and lectures, and is also an authority on landscape gardening. He has managed a castle estate in Ireland, and has been a Reader and Assistant Dean of Cashel Cathedral in the Church of Ireland. He married an internationally well known flautist, Bettine Clemens. Bettine has German nationality. Their home was in the United States, where they built a house in the Amish country.

Ginette was a founder member of the British and Commonwealth Women's Association. This association was founded in 1962 by Lady Mason, the wife of the then British Ambassador to NATO. Its object being essentially for young wives to meet, have lunch and organise various activities. They have a clubhouse and library. For a time Ginette was the librarian and remained a member of the BCWA until she died.

She was also a member of the Ladies Committee which supervised the running of the Victoria Home. The Victoria Home was founded in Paris in commemoration of Queen Victoria's Jubilee in 1887 to provide a dwelling for elderly British women who had lived in France for many years, and whose circumstances did not permit them to have a home of their own or to return to Britain. Many of these women had come to France as governesses to children of French families and stayed in the country on their retirement.

Originally the home owned a house in the fashionable Neuilly suburb in the west of Paris with accommodation for twelve ladies. As the available number of candidates became fewer the home was sold in favour of a flat in Paris to house five occupants. It was during this time that Ginette became Chairman of the Ladies Committee until the home was finally closed in 2003. She much enjoyed this work and was very attached to these old people, one of whom lived to well over a hundred years of age.

At the other end of the scale Ginette was a member of the committee of the Cardew Club which met at the Saint George's Church in Paris. The Club was founded by Prebendary Cardew in the early 1900s when Chaplain of the Scots Kirk in Paris. He provided a home and did much to protect and care for young British girls who were employed as cabaret and stage dancers. Today the Club provides a meeting place for British au pair girls. Ginette eventually succeeded others to become the Chairman and much enjoyed her association with the girls there.

Mario Capra, (right), the Architect of the new head Office at Vitry (below), with Emile Valentin, Henny Gestetner and Jacques Douphy, the Vitry services manager

SICOB Exhibition Paris - visit from Sir Oliver Harvey, British Ambassador, circa 1950

Professional Life

At Gestetner, Henri Bercovitch died of cancer and was succeeded by Charles Buhler. Charles was a grandson of the founder of the Company, David Gestetner. He was working in the Philippine Company when the Japanese invaded the country and was interned for the rest of the war. He suffered considerable hardship but managed to survive. Although I got on well with Charles, my role became less interesting as I was no longer the principal link between France and the Head Office at Tottenham. I seriously thought of leaving but am glad I decided against.

Although Charles had done much to modernise the business and make some good managerial changes, he was a little erratic and not always understood by our French staff. In fact it was during his period of office that the unions, particularly the CGT (Confédération Générale des Travailleurs), became very active in the company. Nevertheless the business continued to prosper and grow. We outgrew our premises at rue du Louvre and acquired a complex in the left-wing-dominated suburb of Vitry-sur-Seine. These premises had been the well known flour mill and factory of the Groult family. They needed a great deal of refurbishing as well as the construction of a new head office block. I was put in charge to oversee this new building. The imposing old flour mill was and still is a listed building but we managed to put it to good use for our stores.

One day Charles, his wife Jeanina and their young son, spent the afternoon with us at our house in Le Vésinet. The

Various Gestetner book matches

Managing Director, Gestetner S.A., 1965
Photo taken in my office at Head Office, Vitry-sur-Seine

next day Jeanina and Philip were to be driven to Nice to be followed later by Charles and myself to attend a Branch Managers' Conference. Charles suggested Ginette should go with them but thankfully she declined. There was a tragic car accident in which Jeanina was seriously injured and Philip and his nurse were killed. Although they had another child neither Charles nor Jeanina fully recovered. Eventually Charles' health deteriorated so much that he was obliged to leave the business.

Emile Valentin, the Sales Manager, was appointed to succeed Charles. Emile took me into his confidence as number two in the French business. Under him the business continued to expand; together we planned the opening of several new branches in France and Francophone Africa. Although we dominated the stencil duplicator market, which was producing handsome profits it was necessary for the Company to develop new products. The company entered the offset market. Offset is a superior printing process compared with the stencil process. Modern offset printers are a development of the ancient lithographic process. They are much more technical than stencil duplicators. It took us a long time to train our sales and technical staff from a low to a higher technical process, but in the face of fierce competition we succeeded in dominating this market in France. Photocopiers, too, were beginning to become a serious threat to the stencil business so the Company acquired a small British company making photocopiers; it was not a great success.

In 1965 Emile, a much respected and loved Managing Director retired. I was appointed to succeed him. I was delighted with this new challenge; being a foreigner and neither a sales nor technical expert I never thought I had a chance. As it turned out, I managed the French Company for seventeen years, much longer than any previous manager. In fact I was the first Manager of the French business to be appointed Président-Directeur-Général. Despite growing

David and Jonathan Gestetner

competition from copiers, particularly Xerox, we managed to beat all previous records in the sale of stencil duplicators and offset machines. Although we had a very shaky start with copiers, we eventually adopted the excellent Mita Japanese copier but the firm did not have the finance to develop sufficiently. We then adopted Ricoh copiers produced in our name. They were, and are, extremely reliable excellent copiers. We were able to hold our own in this market as well competing successfully with Xerox.

When I retired in 1983 we had a staff of nearly 1900 sales, technical and administrative personnel operating from 44 branches. Our annual turnover was nearly six hundred million French francs. We had well maintained our reputation as the jewel in the Gestetner crown as its largest and most profitable subsidiary.

I inherited a wonderful business in France with a magnificent loyal workforce and was lucky enough to have managed it during a large part of the thirty glorious business years of the French economy.

David and Jonathan Gestetner by this time had become joint Managing Directors, the former mainly concerned with the commercial side of the business and the latter the manufacturing side.

1976 was a particularly rewarding year for me. David Gestetner was so delighted with our results that, in view of the fact that Jaguar Cars were not selling well, he suggested I should replace my company car with a Jaguar. I thus acquired the first of three Jaguars. The first quickly became rusty and had many other problems. The second, a Daimler, had the peculiar habit of overflowing from one petrol tank to another leaving a petrol trail behind, which no Jaguar technician could ever solve. It finally broke down on the autoroute. The third was perfect, manufactured after Ford had taken over from Leyland. It was given to me on my retirement. I sold it recently after thirty-two years. I was a bit sad to part with it.

With colleagues relaxing at Moulin Rouge, Paris, after a Gestetner conference. Circa 1965

Olympic Games, Grenoble 1968, showing Offset model 213, one of many to print immediate event results received from IBM. Self with one of the operators.

Celebrating 50th anniversary of Raymond Loewy's association with Gestetner showing Model N°66, the first to be designed by Raymond Loewy in 1929. Left to right: Self, a Loewy partner, Ginette, Jacqueline Gestetner, Jonathan Gestetner, Raymond Loewy, Raymond's wife, a Loewy partner

Gestetner vans

To celebrate my forty years with the Company, David invited me to make a world tour with Ginette visiting Gestetner Companies and agents on the way. We took a month visiting Bangkok, Hong Kong, Bali, Japan, Tahiti, San Francisco, New York, Guadaloupe, and home.

Shortly after that I was honoured to be invited to join the Board of Gestetner Holdings Limited. Subsequently I was given responsibility to the Board for the commercial activities of all our companies in Europe, except Great Britain and Ireland, as well as all subsidiaries and agents in Africa. Israel also came into my orbit. I spent so much time travelling in Europe and Africa that consequently it was necessary to appoint assistant managers for the French Company. Later Pakistan and Sri Lanka were added to my responsibilities. Although I was a director of these subsidiaries I never managed to visit them.

Despite our success in France it was not all honey. At times there was much social unrest in the country. It did not help having our Head Office in the very left wing suburb of Vitry-sur-Seine. This was particularly so in May 1968 when the whole country, universities included, was in turmoil and on strike. I had interminable discussions with the Workers Committee. The Communist Mayor of Vitry encouraged our personnel to stay on strike. For many critical days I was never sure if I would not be detained as a hostage. This was not infrequent elsewhere. I kept a suitcase available in my office just in case and planned how I would escape to meet my chauffeur at a secret rendez-vous.

On such occasions it is very distressing and nerve-wracking to find oneself at odds with those with whom one normally has very good relations. I was never against union representation but at times one felt very much alone, balancing the act to satisfy one's customers, the Company, the shareholders' interests and a proper reward to those who do all the work. Despite some very difficult times the representatives of the personnel were always faultless in their professional duties. We had great respect for each other.

100th Anniversary Dinner. Franco-British Chamber of Commerce with French Prime Minister, Pierre Messmer.

Presenting a cheque of £100,000 to Amadou Mahtar M'Bow, the Director General of UNESCO, on the 100th Anniversary of Gestetner, in 1981

Retirement lunch, Paris 1983, with André Reumont, my successor as Managing Director Gestetner S.A., France, and Rodney Hornstein, who succeeded me on the Board of Gestetner Holdings Ltd. U.K

I always did my best to know everyone in the French business. It was my custom, on arrival at the office, to spend the first hour of the day visiting the workshops, stores and offices to shake the hand of as many as possible and to show interest in their work. I did likewise in my regular visits to branches and the sales teams. I know this was much appreciated and paid dividends in respect and loyalty. I could always rely on them when an extra effort was required.

We tended to consider that our two best customers were the Roman Catholic Church and the Communist Party. Most parishes had a duplicator to produce their parish magazines and other notices. The Communist party was very strong and dominated local politics in much of the country. In towns and villages most local administrations, schools, unions and party offices were under control of the Communists and were Gestetner customers. The Roman Catholics were generally poor so collecting their money was often difficult whereas the Communists always had the money available and paid up promptly.

Nevertheless on a worldwide basis the Catholic Church is a very important customer. To such an extent that whenever Gestetner produced a new model a presentation of the latest production was made to His Holiness the Pope at a private audience at the Vatican. I was twice a member of a delegation to visit Pope Paul VI, a delightfully simple but impressive man. Popes are always at home with Gestetner duplicators as in their less glorious days they had been priests who were accustomed to making use of the stencil process. Despite my Anglican upbringing, shaking hands with the Pope was a thrill to me as I was shaking hands with much of the history of Christianity.

In 1981 Gestetner celebrated its 100th year as a Company. We were still so prosperous in those days that the Board decided to spend a million pounds on some worthwhile project in conjunction with UNESCO. Unfortunately UNESCO displeased some members of the Board so the

Audience with Pope Paul VI, Vatican, February 1975

amount was reduced to one hundred thousand pounds to be applied to update the Braille Process for the Blind. I was delegated to present the cheque to Mr Amadou Mahtar M'Bow, the Director General, at UNESCO Headquarters in Paris.

At 65 I was sad to have to retire and to leave the Company which had given me so much. I am fairly adaptable so was only miserable for one day. Although she sadly had to leave me on the way Ginette and I enjoyed twenty-four years of a very happy retirement taking an active part in the life of the British Community in the Paris Region.

Community Work

Prior to my retirement, despite a fairly heavy work schedule, I gradually became involved in various activities within the British community in the Paris region. I shared much of this work with Ginette. Although she was not always directly involved she was always very supportive and encouraging. In fact I could not have achieved much without her constant support.

Ginette, 2000.

Saint Michael's, The British Embassy Church

The original church, known as the British Embassy Church, was built in 1834 on land purchased in 1833, all of which was personally paid for by Bishop Matthew Luscombe, then chaplain to the British Embassy. It was subsequently bought in 1857 by the Continental and Colonial Church Society (now renamed the Intercontinental Church Society, or ICS), based in Great Britain. This Society appoints the Chaplain.

Shortly after my arrival in Paris I became a member of The British Embassy Church when Bishop George Chambers was Chaplain. He had already reached retirement age but had volunteered to come to Paris to help rebuild the congregation. The current congregation being unable to support the church it was subsidised by the Society for some years before it became self supporting.

George Chambers was a charming person who often gave the impression he was a little vague but this was far from reality as he was disarmingly very much on the ball. As a regular member of the congregation and supported by the Chaplain's Warden, Francis Fairfax-Cholmeley, the Bishop invited me to become a member of the Church Council. It was not long before I was appointed assistant treasurer.

There was no paid staff so all the secretarial work was undertaken by the Bishop's wife helped by various ladies of the congregation, including Ginette. There was no church hall so meetings were held in the Chaplain's flat and sometimes in the Embassy canteen. The church did not even have any toilet facilities. Otherwise this typically Victorian church

*John Morris, Chaplain of St. Michael's, The British Embassy Church,
and the Abbot of the Abbaye de Bec-Hellouin, in 1967*

building was comfortable and well appointed, although the coal fired heating system was not always effective.

We all loved the Bishop and Mrs Chambers, who did so much to rebuild our congregation. We were very sorry when they finally decided to retire to Australia. We later learned the Bishop had returned to Tanganyika to take up a parish, where he died at a very advanced age.

He was succeeded by the Reverend John Morris, with his wife Beryl. There had been a long interregnum before John was appointed, during which time the Society acquired a suitable flat in the rue de Lubeck for the future Chaplain and his family of four children.

I remained a member of the Church Council and on Francis Fairfax-Cholmeley's retirement John invited me to become his Warden. By then the Church's finances had improved and gradually we became self-supporting.

One day I received a visit from the French social security people, who were concerned that we were not paying French Social Security dues. In common with all the foreign churches in Paris, we did not consider we were liable for such charges on the chaplain's stipend and our first newly appointed paid church secretary. It was decreed we must comply, so we were duly required to regularise our situation, to keep appropriate accounts and to make the necessary returns.

This was quite a blow to our finances. It was not long before both the official treasurer and myself were replaced by John Hall, a chartered accountant, to cope with the growing needs of fund raising, collections and all manner of financial matters. John was most efficient at this and served the church in this capacity for many years. Together with his wife Claudia they were, and still are, very devout and respected members of our congregation.

Although the Chaplain was not a member of the British Embassy staff he had privileged access to the Embassy commissary, free petrol and other advantages — a very welcome subsidy.

During John's incumbency the congregation grew considerably. He and Beryl were very generous in welcoming members to their flat for meetings; in fact it really became the church hall. The young wives group and the young people's Sunday tea parties became extremely popular.

It was customary for the Ambassador and his family to attend services. They had reserved seats in the Ambassador's box on the first floor at the west end overlooking the congregation. Together with my fellow churchwardens it was our duty to escort the Ambassador to the lectern to read the lesson.

I was quite comfortable with our church services which were based on the traditional 1662 Anglican prayer book as this was similar to all other services I had attended in my life so far.

John Morris was chaplain between 1956 and 1969 before being called to become Vicar of Holy Trinity Brompton.

One of the highlights of John's chaplaincy was the first official visit of an Anglican Archbishop of Canterbury, Michael Ramsey, to France since the Reformation. John — together with myself and my fellow churchwarden, Jack Wicker — had the privilege of welcoming the Archbishop by escorting him in procession from the British Embassy to the Embassy Church, accompanied by representatives of the Roman Catholic and Orthodox churches and other dignitaries.

At the end of his visit to France several of us accompanied the Archbishop to the Abbey of Bec-Hellouin in Normandy for a special service. This famous Abbey, founded in the XIth Century, had been a great seat of Christian learning and had provided three early Archbishops of Canterbury: Lefranc, Anselm and Thomas à Becket.

The Archbishop stayed the night in the monastery, and, as the story goes, was provided with porridge at breakfast by the Benedictine monks. The Archbishop felt it had a strange taste and inquired what it was made of. They told him it was laced with calvados, the traditional Norman apple juice spirit. Ramsey declined a second helping.

British Embassy Church, Paris

The Chaplain and Churchwardens
wish to inform you that this Church will be honoured
by the presence of

His Grace The Archbishop of Canterbury

at Evensong on Sunday, 23rd April

at 7 p.m.

when he will preach the sermon.

This card will ensure a seat for

Mr & Mrs Gyles Longley

R.S.V.P.

Done

Mr. and Mrs. Longley

Her Britannic Majesty's Ambassador

and Lady Reilly

at Home
in honour of the Most Rev. the Lord
Archbishop of Canterbury and Mrs. Ramsey

Saturday, 22 April

11.45 - 13.00

39 rue du Faubourg St. Honoré

Social Secretary

R.S.V.P

The Archbishop of Canterbury visiting the Embassy Church, 1967

Procession from the Embassy to the Embassy Church with Archbishop Michael Ramsey, 1967

The Embassy Church building had suffered during the war and much needed to be done to restore it. Many solutions were examined but none of them were satisfactory and in any case we did not have the available funds. The other Parisian Anglican church, St George's, situated near the Arc de Triomphe had similar problems. St George's tradition is Anglo-Catholic, whereas the Embassy church has an Evangelical tradition. Together with Frank Laws-Johnson, the chairman of the organisation which owned St. George's, we formed the Joint Anglican Committee in agreement with John Morris and the Church Council.

The object was to examine the possibility of pooling our resources, based on the high value of the sites which the churches occupied, and to build a common church centre, either on one of the two existing sites, or at another suitable location. It was not the intention to combine the two traditions. Although John was much in favour of the idea he felt that he had served long enough and wished to move on, but he encouraged us to pursue the matter. During the interregnum following John's withdrawal, our discussions advanced sufficiently for us to be prepared to put the question of the principal of the scheme to our respective congregations. The diocese agreed in principal providing the two congregations voted sixty per cent in favour. St. George's held their vote and obtained more than 60% in favour. It was not possible for us to hold our vote until a new Chaplain had been appointed.

In due course we interviewed The Reverend Eric McLellan as prospective candidate for the post. He had been proposed by the ICS and had been approved by the Archbishop of Canterbury, the Bishop of London and the Suffragan Bishop of Fulham. Eric assured us he was happy to go ahead with the scheme, provided that the congregation attained the required vote of 60% in favour, so we accepted his application to be our new Chaplain.

In the meantime matters had become more complicated as the nearby Methodist Church, which also had restoration problems, asked to take part in the scheme. Whilst they were quite happy for their very small congregation to worship at St Michael's they wanted to be equal partners in any scheme.

The time came for St Michael's to hold its vote on the principle of a joint church centre. A meeting was held in the British Embassy canteen. The Ambassador, Sir Christopher Soames and his wife Mary were present. They were both ardent supporters of the proposal. During the meeting there were some unfortunate remarks made by opponents of the proposal which were insulting to the Ambassador. The vote was duly taken. Although it was in favour it failed to attain the required 60% by a very small margin.

The following day I was summoned, together with my two fellow churchwardens, Jack Wicker and Brian Cordery, to the Ambassador's office at the Embassy to be told that we were no longer permitted to retain the title 'The British Embassy Church'. Furthermore all Embassy privileges for the Chaplain would cease forthwith. The Ambassador was furious at the manner in which the Chaplain had conducted the meeting as he felt he had sabotaged the scheme.

Although I had been one of the originators of the scheme I also became *persona non grata* with the Ambassador, who let it be known he would never sit at the same table with me. As it happens he did sit next to me; I became President of the British Chamber of Commerce and he often attended our luncheons. He had the grace to apologise to me for his attitude following the meeting, but he never put his foot in the church again. The incident resulted in several members leaving St. Michael's to join other churches in the Paris region.

I continued as Chaplain's warden but relations with Eric were understandably estranged so we parted company and I was not re-elected to the Church Council. The Church then decided to develop its own site. The development provided us with a less attractive but modern church with space for meetings, offices and many other amenities as well as the Chaplain's flat. It was completed in 1975.

I was naturally very disappointed that the combined church centre scheme could not be achieved. Despite all the anguish it was God's wish that it would not be so. St Michael's, as well as St George's which also developed its own site, has continued to grow and to prosper since those difficult days. Despite my feelings at the time I have remained a faithful member of St Michael's.

Although the Church had adopted the name of Saint Michael as its patron Saint in addition to that of the Embassy Church some years beforehand, it was not until 1969 that the former Archbishop of Canterbury, Dr. Coggan, visited Paris to consecrate the Church in the name of Saint Michael.

During Eric McLellan's time the Series 2 order of service was introduced. This of course was to bring worship into line with modern English but for me it lost the beauty of the 1662 Book of Common Prayer.

Since St Michael's became my Church in 1946, I have known eight Chaplains, all of whom have made significant contributions to the quality of worship and strength of Christian faith in Paris and beyond. During this time several friends and members of St Michael's have found their vocation there and taken up Holy Orders. Some people come to France for relatively short periods of time so the congregation is constantly changing and has an annual turnover of some 60%. I am now the doyen. Although the congregation is primarily English speaking it is composed of several different nationalities. There are services in French and Tamil for those who prefer.

Throughout my more than sixty-six years in this country St Michael's Church has been my spiritual home, a constant haven of love and spiritual inspiration.

The Royal British Legion, Paris Branch

I became a member of the Paris Branch of the Royal British Legion (RBL) soon after arriving in Paris in 1946.

The Branch claims to be the oldest branch of the RBL organisation as it was formed by a group of World War veterans in Paris just prior to the formation of the Legion by Earl Haig in Great Britain.

Essentially the Legion is a charitable organisation which raises money from different sources, the most important of which is the annual Poppy Appeal. All money collected for the Poppy Appeal is spent in aid of persons in need, or their dependents, who have served in Her Britannic Majesty's Forces. The Legion owns and runs several homes and other institutions for the benefit of ex-service personnel.

All Legion branches are licensed by the United Kingdom Headquarters and operate under the conditions of the Royal Charter. The Paris Branch also runs a Club at its headquarters in the rue d'Acacias in Paris. Not all Legion branches run clubs which are managed separately and have to be self-financing. Clubs cannot be financed in anyway from the Legion's charitable funds.

The Poppy Appeal is centred around Armistice Day, 11th November, when the Queen attends a service at Westminster Abbey.

Since it was inaugurated by Edward, Prince of Wales, in 1924, the Paris Branch has, every year except for 1939-1945, celebrated Armistice Day at Notre Dame Cathedral in Paris. In a very moving service, the British Ambassador reads the lesson, and the Chairman cites the Oration. The Cathédral is reserved for the British Community that day and is always packed. The service is preceded by a procession of the British clergy from churches in the Paris region, together with the combined British choirs, the standard bearers of British, French and other international veterans associations, accompanied by a piper. The service is conducted in English with a welcome from the Cathédral Chancellor. The two-minute silence is preceded by a bugler sounding the Last Post followed by the Reveille. A prelude is played on the grand organ and invariably Land of Hope and Glory as the postlude. The Legion is very grateful to the Embassy and the Cathédral authorities for their help in the organisation and for the security arrangements.

Another annual event is the laying of a Poppy wreath on the Tombeau du Soldat Inconnu (the French Unknown Soldier) on the 4th August at the Arc de Triomphe—a ceremony which has been enacted every year since 1924. The Chairman leads a procession of French and British dignitaries for the ceremony of Rekindling the Flame under the Arc. Again there is a procession of many standard bearers and the accompaniment of a French military band playing both National Anthems and other appropriate music. The Oration is again cited followed by a two minute silence.

I became a member of the branch committee in the 1970s and was elected Chairman in May 1994 until January 1996. One of the highlights during my term of office was the celebration of the fiftieth anniversary of VE-Day on 8th May 1995. We held a drumhead service in the grounds of the Standard Athletic Club in the forest of Meudon. I had never become a member of this club, although it was founded in 1890 for British families in the Paris region. It has a fine clubhouse, bar and billiards, restaurant, gym and changing rooms. There are a swimming pool, several tennis courts, a cricket ground and other sporting facilities.

The VE-Day celebration was very much an Allied affair open to all members of the British Community

Wreath laying, Royal British Legion, Arc de Triomphe, 1995

and delegations from many Commonwealth and Allied countries, including the Americans and Russians.

It was sponsored by the British Community Committee, under the Presidency of Jan Mitchell. It was organised by the Legion Paris Branch, under my Chairmanship, in association with many organisations such as the British Embassy, the British Churches, the British Commonwealth Womens Association (BCWA), the British School of Paris, the International Players, both the Royal Naval and Royal Air Force Associations, the Scouts and several others. The British Ambassador, Sir Christopher Mallaby together with Mrs Pamela Harriman, the American Ambassador, presided over the event with the presence of the local French Prefect and many other dignitaries. The French Army lent marquee tents, the British Community organised a barbecue, and the British School of Paris Orchestra played excellently. We had a wonderful steel band concert from the Philadelphia Girls High School who were visiting Paris at the time. We even had the services of the Sergeant-Major of one of the Guards regiments in full dress to marshall our parade. It was a perfect summer's day ending with an enormous bonfire and firework display, followed by dancing.

It took months to prepare by an *ad hoc* committee chaired by my friend Gerald Joury, who did a remarkable job, assisted by the Branch Secretary, Janet Warby and her husband Roger, our Parade Marshall, and other members of the Branch.

Every year since about 1985 the Royal British Legion in London has organised a sponsored cycle rally from Greenwich to Paris ending up for a ceremony at the Arc de Triomphe. It started from small beginnings; now several hundred cyclists take part, raising quite considerable sums of money for the Poppy Appeal. I had the privilege of organising the Paris end of the first rally although much of the work was undertaken by French committee member, Colonel Jazir, who arranged for the motor cycle escort, staging posts en route, and the presence of a military band for the ceremony at the Arc. It terminated by a reception by the French Army at Les Invalides, the equivalent of the Chelsea Hospital. Colonel Jazir is a member of the Comité de la Flamme and President of the French Parachute veterans.

I am still involved with the Legion as Honorary President of the Paris Branch.

Joint Dinner of the French and British Chambers of Commerce, Hilton Hotel, London, 1973. From left to right: Sir Patrick Reilly, President of the London Chamber of Commerce, ex-British Ambassador in Paris; Mme Nicole Glain (wife of Jacques Glain, President of the French Chamber of Commerce in Great Britain), self, president of the British Chamber of Commerce in France; Lady Douglas Home; S.E. Beaumarchais, French Ambassador; Rt. Hon. Sir Alex Douglas Home, Foreign Secretary.

As President of the Franco-British Chamber, greeting François Ceyrac,
Président Patronat Français, October 1975

The British Chamber of Commerce and Industry in France

By 1873 Victoria had been on the throne of the United Kingdom since 1837. Patrice de MacMahon was newly appointed Chief of State of the French Republic. A Treaty of Free Trade was signed between Britain and France. Almost immediately, a group of twenty-three British businessmen, mainly cloth importers from the world-famous mills, founded the Franco-British Chamber of Commerce, with the motto *Free Trade, Peace, and Goodwill among Nations*, to protect the interests of these traders in the application of the treaty.

My Company, Gestetner, had been a leading member of the Chamber for many years, and I regularly attended Chamber functions. It was in 1962, under the Chairmanship of H. C. Talbot that I was appointed a Director of the Chamber. In 1970 I was appointed Vice-President, and then President in 1972, succeeding David Goodchild, C.B.E. It was an exciting time, thanks to the efforts of Edward Heath, then Prime Minister, well backed up by the British Ambassador, Sir Christopher Soames. The French President, General de Gaulle, agreed to support Great Britain's application to join the European Union or Common Market.

The Chamber is an independent organisation financed by British and French companies trading between the two countries. It receives no outside subvention. It also relies on the income from their well-established Commercial English Language Examinations. The Chamber's magazine *Cross Channel Trade* gave information on Member Company activities, and highlighted the views of the Chamber on trade

COBCOE Assembly, Madrid, 1986. An audience with King Juan Carlos.

between France and The United Kingdom. The Chamber has very strong links with the Embassy. I liaised frequently with the Ambassador, Sir Christopher Soames, and his successor, Sir Edward Tomkins, as well as the Commercial Minister, Ronald Arculus. One of my last initiatives as President was to write to the Prime Minister, Harold Wilson, to bring his attention to the situation of British Companies exporting to France, should Britain leave the Common Market. The reply from the Prime Minister was reassuring and in 1975, by referendum, Britain voted to remain in the Common Market.

In conjunction with the Board of Trade and the British Embassy we organised British Weeks in various cities in France. A British Week was an occasion for companies to display their goods as well as for various conferences with local Chambers of Commerce and other authorities. These occasions were quite exhausting with speeches and interviews on local radio and television. The first British week was held in Lille and was inaugurated by Sir Christopher Soames.

In 1972 the Chamber celebrated the 100th anniversary of its foundation with a dinner to which I invited Monsieur Pierre Messmer, the French Prime Minister, to be our guest of honour.

It is customary to hold the Presidency of the Chamber for two years; I handed over to my successor, Eustace Balfour, but remained a Vice-President for a further two years and thereafter continued as a Director until my retirement in 1983.

After retirement I remained a Vice-President of The Council of British Chambers of Commerce in Europe (COBCOE). The object is to discuss and co-ordinate matters relating to the European Chambers in conjunction with the Board of Trade. Meetings were held in a different country each year. When we held the annual congress in Madrid we were received by King Juan Carlos at the Royal Palace.

In 1976 I was appointed Commander in the Order of the British Empire (CBE) for my services to the British Community in France. I received my award from the hands of Her Majesty at an investiture at Buckingham Palace.

Buckingham Palace Investiture, C.B.E., with Ginette and Biddy, 1977.

The Trustees of the Hertford British Hospital, 2006. Centre, 9th Marquess of Hertford (Patron) with Marchioness on left

The Hertford British Hospital

The Hospital was founded in 1879, by Sir Richard Wallace, and named The Hertford British Hospital in memory of his putative father, the 4th Marquess of Hertford. The last hundred years have seen considerable change in the activities of the Hospital. From the early days, the Hospital had been under-financed, receiving no subventions from either the British or French governments. Initially only for British residents, it now receives a high percentage of French patients, always maintaining an excellent medical reputation.

During his term of office The President of the Chamber of Commerce automatically becomes a trustee of the Hospital. Accordingly in 1972 I was co-opted and attended my first Council Meeting.

The situation was critical. The original Hospital building, with its large wards, was no longer practical and there was no further funding available to refurbish the building. After a vote to close the Hospital, the situation was reversed by a movement of the staff and the Communist Mayor of Levallois-Perret, Monsieur Parfait Jans, who obtained the agreement of the DDASS (Direction Départementale des Affaires Sanitaires et Sociales) to change the status of the Hospital from a privately run Clinic to be a Private Hospital, financed by the French authorities.

The next step was to try and rebuild the hospital, which could only be achieved through the aid of the French Health authorities. Fortunately the Ambassador, Sir Nicolas

Henderson, took a keen interest in the future of the Hospital, and liaised with the Health Minister, Madame Simone Veil, so that a new hospital building was financed entirely by the French State. Our patron, Queen Elizabeth the Queen Mother, opened the new hospital building in 1982.

We then had to decide how to develop the now empty original Hospital building. With David Goodchild, then Chairman of the Hospital Corporation, we planned for the Charity to have available 6200 sq. metres of prime office space. This was realised by converting the original hospital premises, commonly known as the 'Cathedral' and building two extra wings in the garden. We were not permitted to demolish the 'Cathedral' as it is a listed building.

As I was newly retired from business in 1983 David Goodchild invited me to oversee this new stage of development of the Hospital and its site. We appointed the firm Weatheral, Green and Smith as consultants to help us manage the project — appointing an architect, planning, arranging with banks for finance, examining estimates and appointing the builders. The realisation of this project considerably increased the income of the Hospital Trust, thus enabling it to secure the objects for which it was founded. The first tenant was the French branch of the worldwide advertising agency, McCann Erickson, who remained for the next twenty years. Nevertheless the Trust was saddled with a heavy debt which has only recently been cleared; income is only now available for further improvements and facilities. The Hospital has always been well known for its excellent maternity services; indeed my wife Ginette and her sister were born there so I am the last to complain.

Some six years after I became a Trustee, I was called on to be Chairman of the Management Committee. The newly appointed Chairman, Edward Lace, was forced to resign through ill health, and I took on the task for one year, before Robin Peat succeeded me in 1991. I remained a Trustee until my 90th year when I felt it was time to give up.

The Council of the Hospital Trustees is made up of some

twenty devoted members of the British Community and in my over 35 years as one of them we have managed the affairs of the Trust through some very difficult times. Since I have retired the Hospital has amalgamated with the other local hospital in the town of Levallois-Perret, the Hopital de Perpétuel Secours, to become L'Institut Hospitalier Franco-Britannique. The government of the Hospital is shared by the two hospital units with the Hertford section being responsible for the maternity and pediatrics departments. Two thousand five hundredd babies are now born there annually.

As a member of the Hertford British Hospital Association, I regularly attend the Annual General Meeting of the Hertford British Hospital Corporation. This is a charitable organisation incorporated in England and supervised by the Charity Commissioners in London.

Other Activities

Apart from the above, I am, or have been, involved in a number of other activities.

For a number of years I was a member of the governing committee of the Victoria Home until it closed. Ginette had already been a member for some time in her capacity as a member of the Ladies Committee.

Since my retirement it has always been a pleasure to be a member of the 'Amicale des Anciens de Gestetner France et du Groupe Ricoh'. It was originally formed as a friendly association open to all ex-employees of Gestetner France and later to those of the photocopier subsidiary of the Ricoh Group (which had acquired the Gestetner business some years after I had retired). The Association arranges for an annual lunch in the Paris region and an annual three day visit to an attractive area in France.

I am not in any way an official of this organisation but it is for me an immense joy to spend some time with old colleagues of every rank in the firm, many of whom I had worked with in the past. Gestetner has always had a wonderful 'esprit de corps' which continues in retirement. I am not the oldest member: one of our number will be a hale and hearty 100 years old by the time these memoirs are published.

I became a member of the British Luncheon (1916) in 1969. The Association is open to prominent men and women living in the Paris Region. It has a limited membership at present fixed at 105 including members of the British Diplomatic

Master of Fidelity Lodge N°10 and his Lady Opening the Ball, Ladies Night , October 1961

Corps and the British Clergy in the Paris region. Its origins evolved during the 1914-18 War as the Ambassador's Advisory Committee on Exemptions when the Conscription Act came into force. The Committee often met for lunch to discuss their business and after the war continued to do so; thus the British Luncheon (1916) came into being. Today members meet once a month for lunch at the Cercle Interalliée in the Rue du Faubourg Saint Honoré. No speeches are permitted except for the Christmas lunch when spouses and friends are invited and the President makes a short speech generally followed by the current Ambassador giving an account of Franco-British relations during the past year. The President is elected each year at a lunch of Past Presidents. I was elected President in 1980.

For most of my time in France I have been a member of the Royal Society of Saint George, Paris Branch, and was for some years a member of the Committee. The object of the Society is to promote England and all that is English. There is an annual President's cocktail party, and a picnic lunch at the Longchamp racecourse for the meeting a week or so before the Prix de l'Arc de Triomphe. Occasionally there are outings to places of interest in the Paris area.

I became a Freemason in France in 1953. My father-in-law had been a Mason before WW2; my brother-in-law had joined him shortly after the war. Naturally it was not long before I decided to join them too. Ginette's mother and her sister were all delighted as they would then have evenings together when all the family men were out doing their 'boy scouts' duties' as they liked to describe our masonic evenings. Accordingly I was initiated into Fidelity Lodge No 10, an English-speaking Lodge within the Obedience of the Grande Loge Nationale Française (GLNF). At the time of writing, the GLNF is the only masonic obedience in France which is recognised by the United Grand Lodges of England (UGLE), the accepted authority on Regular Freemasonry throughout the world. 'Regular' requires adhering to a strict discipline of moral behaviour towards all mankind, regardless of nationality, creed or race, whether or not a fellow freemason. Religion and politics are barred from discussion within a Lodge. Women are not admitted to be become members of Regular Lodges. Freemasonry is not a religion, but one cannot be a member unless one is a believer in God, from whom all goodness emanates, and one who accepts the Bible as the sacred law to guide one's conduct in life. Masonry originated from the symbolism relating to the tools and customs of the builders of the great Temple of Jerusalem, Cathedrals and other important buildings in ancient times. Although some rituals may give that impression, Masonry is not a secret society. Literature on masonic ritual and practice are readily available at most bookshops. Brotherly Love, Charity and Truth are the basic tenets of Masonry.

Unfortunately Freemasonry is not looked on with favour in many circles. In some countries it is forbidden. In some religious circles it also not acceptable. This is owing to non-regular Obediences indulging in political or unacceptable religious discussion. Freemasons are sometime persecuted, and in Nazi Germany were sent to the gas chambers.

Although I am no longer an active member of my Lodge I have enjoyed many years of excellent fellowship as a Freemason. I was twice Master of my Lodge and attained high rank in the Obedience. Going through the stages of Initiation, passing to the rank of Fellow Craft, then raising to become a Master Mason, and later to Master of the Lodge requires much hard work, learning the long complex rituals by heart and being able to recite them without a mistake when called upon to do so.

In 1968 David Gestetner and Bill François, Manager of the Belgian Company, proposed me to become a Member of the Confrérie des Chevaliers du Tastevin. I was duly admitted as a Chevalier at a Chapitre (Chapter) ceremony followed by dinner at the well restored ancient Cistercian Abbey of the Château du Clos de Vougeot, in the celebrated vineyard of

Ceremony of Confrérie des Chevaliers du Tastevin, 2008

that name. The object of the Confrerie is to promote Burgundy wines. It is open to anyone and attracts membership from all over the world.

There are about eighteen Chapitres a year at the Château, when about five hundred guests in evening dress assemble for a colourful ceremony of initiation. This is followed by a dinner in the ancient wine cellars, during which there are witty speeches, burgundy drinking songs, music and poetry.

The dinners are sumptuous, with six courses, each accompanied with its appropriate wine. One of the courses being 'oeufs meurette' (two soft boiled eggs in a burgundy sauce). The marvel is that one thousand warm soft boiled eggs are served within a few minutes.

Not only the service is impeccable but the Confrérie also arranges buses to pick up the guests at their hotels in the region and to bring them back in a mellow mood at the end of the festivities.

Charles' 90th Birthday at Barber's Hall, London. Charles, self, Biddy, Dennis

Biddy in her retirement home, 2010

Afterthoughts

I have much for which to be thankful, not the least the good fortune to be blessed with relatively good health, despite two open heart by-pass operations. Six years ago my pulse rate was so low I could hardly do anything without feeling utterly exhausted. There was a miraculous recovery when I had a pace-maker fitted. I did not start leaping around but it did made life worth living again.

In anyone's life there are regrets. In my case I regret not having taken sufficient advantage of my education. Although not cut out to be a student, I could have done better.

Above all for both Ginette and I our saddest regret was not to have any children. Dear Ginette went through all the process of trying to find the cause until the finger was pointed at me. It turned out that I was the culprit. Who knows, perhaps my sterility was the result of my mother's smoking, or the result of having mumps when I was a kid. I bear no grudge against anyone that I drew the unlucky ticket. It took us a little while to adjust to this blow to our ambition to have several children but our love for each other never wavered. A pity as Ginette was so good with children. We did consider adoption and started the process but for various reasons did not pursue the matter.

The English and the French do not have much natural affinity for each other. There is a sort of love/hate relationship between the two peoples nurtured by their respective histories. Despite this there are countless very successful Franco-British partnerships in business and in marriage.

Franco-British marriages are some of the most successful, being enriched by taking advantage of both cultures.

It is not easy to make intimate French friends but when one does the relationship is most rewarding.

As far as my experience is concerned the French are hard working and loyal. What is more they do not stop for tea for a chat. However I am beginning to wonder if things are not changing with the no smoking ban in offices. Taking time to come out of the office into the street to give you a whiff of secondary smoke as you pass by may cost as much as the British tea break.

Inevitably the longer one lives one loses a great many family members as well as friends, comrades and colleagues on the way. It is they who have shaped one's life and to whom one owes a debt of gratitude. Thankfully I have found wonderful new friends to take their place.

Throughout my life, despite failures, I have done my best to be honest and fair and to love my neighbour, even if I dislike him.

I am glad I did not take on a career with the local Beckenham electricity showroom!

Ginette and I

Bibliography

A Duty to Serve Tonbridge School and the 1939-45 War - *David Walsh* (Third Millenium Publishing - 2011)

A Full Life - *Lt-Gen: Sir Brian Horrocks* (Collins-Fontana Books - 1962)

A History of Tonbridge School - *D.C.Somervell* (Faber and Faber)

El Alamein - *Michael Carver* (B.T.Batsford 1962)

Italy's Sorrow - *James Holland* (Harpers Press 2008)

Memories of Saint Michael's - *John Hall* (2007)

Pedigree of The Hovenden Family *compiled by Robert Hovenden F.S.A.* (Printed privately by Mitchell Hughes & Clarke 1908)

Rommel - *Desmond Young* (Collins-Fontana Books 1955)

Salerno - *Eric Morris* (Hutchinson 1993)

Sir Richard Wallace - *Peter Howard* (The Grimsay Press 2009)

The Reconnaissance Journal - *Lt. J.L.Taylor* (Withy Grove Press - 1945)

The Origins of Stencil Duplicating - *W.B.Proudfoot* (Hutchinson 1972)

The Rommel Papers - *Liddell Hart* (Harcourt, Brace, and Company 1953)

This Band of Brothers - *Jeremy Taylor* (The White Swan Press -1947)

Tonbridge School Register 1920-1985 - *T.C.Cobb* - 1986

Index